GROWING UP IN
WARTIME UXBRIDGE

Royal Air Force Uxbridge

Wartime Operations Centre

HQ No 11 Group Fighter Command 1936-1958

GROWING UP IN
WARTIME UXBRIDGE

JAMES SKINNER

This book is dedicated to all those men and women whose sacrifice made it possible for us to continue growing up in peacetime.

Front Cover: Local Home Guard units formed part of a 'Wings For Victory' parade through Uxbridge on 6 March 1943.

Back Cover, left: The author aged nine. *Right:* Yiewsley housewives in Castle Avenue responding to the call to save food scraps for pigs and poultry. The council's collector (left) is Benny Jones.

Frontispiece: Front cover of the brochure for visitors to the Operations Room in peacetime.

First published 2008
Reprinted 2019

Tempus Publishing, The History Press
97 St George's Place, Cheltenham,
Gloucestershire, GL50 3QB
www.thehistorypress.co.uk
Tempus Publishing is an imprint of The History Press
© James Skinner, 2008

The right of James Skinner to be identified as the Author of this work has been asserted in accordance with the Copyrights, Designs and Patents Act 1988.

All rights reserved. No part of this book may be reprinted or reproduced or utilised in any form or by any electronic, mechanical or other means, now known or hereafter invented, including photocopying and recording, or in any information storage or retrieval system, without the permission in writing from the Publishers.

British Library Cataloguing in Publication Data.
A catalogue record for this book is available from the British Library.

ISBN 978 0 7524 4543 4

Typesetting and origination by The History Press
Printed in Great Britain by TJ International Ltd, Padstow, Cornwall.

Contents

	Acknowledgements	6
	Introduction	7
one	The Pre-War Years	9
	An Early Bereavement	13
	Schooldays	16
	Shopping Around	17
	The Outdoor Life	21
	Royal Celebrations	30
	The Munich Crisis	45
two	The War Years	47
	Preparing for War	48
	Evacuation	49
	The Miracle of Dunkirk	64
	The Battle of Britain	70
	Peril on the Sea	72
	The Blitz	81
	Families of War	82
	D-Day and Doodlebugs	103
	Peace at Last	107
three	The Post-War Years	113
	Victory Celebrations	114
	Life in the RAF	115
	Back in Civvy Street	121
	Wedding Bells	126
	New Beginnings	127

Acknowledgements

Again I am indebted to the *Uxbridge Gazette* for the loan of archive material and for granting permission to reproduce it in this book.

And, as always, my grateful thanks are due to Carolynne Cotton, Gwyn Jones and Richard Daniels of the Heritage Department, Uxbridge Central Library for their help and the loan of their photographs.

My sincere thanks also to the following individuals for providing me with information, and for generously allowing me to use their personal photographs: Chris Wren (former curator of the RAF Museum) Ken Pearce, Dr R.T. Smith, Joyce Burden, Patrick and Sheila Burgoyne, Eva Adnett, Peter Koenig, Maureen and Philip Sherwood, Audrey Beasley, Val Culmer, Bryan Williams, Alan Noad, Brian Moores, Gareth Owen, Robert Caughey, Agnes Eggleston, Maureen Franklin, Pamela Holden, Vivienne Drewett, Audrey and Michael Skinner, Alan Johnston.

Finally, a special thank you to Elaine Verweymeren for processing my manuscript.

Introduction

Although the title *Growing Up In Wartime Uxbridge* is self-explanatory, and would not appear to need an introduction, I am taking this opportunity to sketch a broad outline of the book's format.

The main body of the work is contained in the middle chapter and lives up to its title, since it focuses on the Second World War years of 1939-1945. However, by way of added interest, I decided to preface this with an opening chapter dealing with the previous decade. From a child's viewpoint, those pre-war years of the 1930s were full of carefree, halcyon days when the sun always seemed to shine. But before anyone protests about that statement, let me hastily add that for many people, the 1930s were, regrettably, quite the opposite. It was a time for the 'haves' and the 'have nots'; to quote from Dickens 'It was the best of times: It was the worst of times'.

So, having started with a prologue, I thought it appropriate to round off the book with a shorter final chapter on the post-war period up to the end of the 1940s.

Finally, I hope that readers will bear with me if I complete these introductory notes with a brief personal reference to my family background, especially in view of my forebears' involvement with the military and previous wartimes.

My father (also James) served with the RASC (Royal Army Service Corps) during the First World War, being mentioned in dispatches in 1917, and my grandfather (another James) was a Lieutenant in the 45th regiment of the British Army. My great grandfather was a Major who commanded the Indian 14th Irregular Cavalry, while my great great grandfather, Col James Skinner, CB (1778-1841) was the founder of the illustrious Skinner's Horse Cavalry Regiment (later the First Duke of York's Own Skinner's Horse).

However, despite coming from a long line of military men, I was the first to break with the family's Army tradition when I joined the RAF early in 1946.

Thankfully, I was also the first in the line not to have been actively engaged in warfare.

Cover of the programme of events during Warship Week 1942. Uxbridge adopted the Destroyer HMS *Intrepid* which unfortunately sank in October 1943.

one

The Pre-War Years

On a bleak, midwinter day in January, 1928, a cross-channel ferry from Calais was riding on a storm-tossed sea, carrying my mother back to England. And she was carrying me. After living in France for eighteen months, she wanted me to be born in this country, but was obliged to make the journey alone as my father could not leave due to work commitments.

After serving in France during the First World War, my father returned home, not to the 'land fit for heroes to live in' as the politicians had promised, but to a country reeling from mass unemployment, widespread strikes, food shortages, lawlessness and a general feeling of despair. The unemployment figure soon topped the one million mark – over two thirds being ex-servicemen. With no prospects of a job, he went back to France, finding employment with the BRCS (British Red Cross Society) Mobile Unit and the War Graves Commission. He worked around Lille and Arras for eight years, during which time he met my mother in Uxbridge on one of his leaves.

I first saw the light of day at No. 6 Cleveland Road, the nursing home run by sisters Hilda and Maud Franklin, before being taken home to How's Road, where my mother lived with her parents. The twenty Edwardian terraced houses in the road and eleven others in adjoining How's Close were built in 1906 on the site of a large apple orchard. They were the 'three up, three down' type with bathrooms (but no hot water); tiny gardens with outside toilets, and no electricity. Heating was provided by fireplaces in every room.

Both roads and paths were gravel surfaced, prone to potholes that became quagmires in winter and dust bowls in summer. They stayed that way until 1936 when tarmac surfaces were laid along with paving slabs on the paths.

Living with parents and grandparents was an enjoyable experience, even if it meant being spoilt. My father had returned to England soon after my arrival on the scene, and I have fond

Another wartime. My father serving with the Royal Army Service Corps in France, c.1917.

Right: At the same time my mother enlisted in the Women's Royal Air Force at Uxbridge.

Below: My father's certificate for being mentioned in dispatches, signed by Winston Churchill, Secretary of State for War.

The War of 1914-1918.

Army Service Corps

No. MS/5007 Pte. (A/L/C.) J. Skinner

was mentioned in a Despatch from

Field Marshal Sir Douglas Haig, G.C.B., G.C.V.O., K.C.I.E.

dated 9th April 1917

for gallant and distinguished services in the Field.

I have it in command from the King to record His Majesty's high appreciation of the services rendered.

Winston S. Churchill

War Office
Whitehall, S.W.
1st March 1919.

Secretary of State for War.

memories of him and my grandfather joining in my childhood games, especially when I careered round the living room on a baby tricycle followed by one of them on a wooden horse and the other on a similar toy on wheels.

My grandfather, Walter Turton, a keen musician, had played the bass euphonium in the Uxbridge and Hillingdon Prize Band for thirty-seven years. One of their regular engagements was a twice-weekly concert in the Fassnidge Recreation Ground. He was also a respected member of the Uxbridge Volunteer Fire Brigade for fifteen years, and became something of a local hero, when in April 1924 a mystery fire broke out at the top of a 450-ft aerial mast at Northolt Post Office Wireless Station. Appeals for assistance were made to several local Fire Brigades who, according to *The Evening News* report, felt obliged to decline, considering 'that it was a job for steeplejacks, not firemen'. Nevertheless, when the Uxbridge Brigade arrived on the scene my grandfather volunteered, along with two colleagues, F.C. Wright and R. Crook, to make the ascent. To quote again from *The Evening News*, 'With fire appliances on their backs it took them nearly an hour to climb the mast, and on reaching the top they hacked away the burning wood support – it was well above the aerial wires – with their axes'. Shortly afterwards the three volunteers became the proud recipients of letters of commendation from the Postmaster General, and their photographs appeared in the *Daily Mirror* with the caption 'Steeplejack Firemen'.

In view of his 450-ft climb, it was cruelly ironic that seven years later he should lose his life falling from 35ft up – and even worse – that it should be during a practice fire drill. It was the evening of 28 May 1931, and a dozen members of the brigade were engaged in a routine escape drill at Kings Mill, Denham. Suddenly my grandfather appeared to lose his footing at the top

Right: My maternal grandfather Walter Turton, a bandsman for thirty-seven years with Uxbridge and Hillingdon Prize Band.

Opposite above: My birthplace – the Nursing Home at No. 6 Cleveland Road.

Opposite below: My home for twenty-one years at No. 18 How's Road. The iron gate posts remain, but the railings were removed to aid the war effort.

The bandstand in Fassnidge Park, the venue for twice-weekly band concerts during summertime.

Kings Mill by the River Colne at Denham, where my grandfather met with his fatal accident.

of the ladder and while reaching for the Davy escape apparatus, fell to the ground. On arrival at Hillingdon Hospital he was examined by the then head, Dr 'Jock' Rutherford, who found a fractured pelvis, arm, femur, and several broken ribs. He died on the following morning, and the coroner's report indicated that he had remained lucid and never lost consciousness.

On 2 June, after a Requiem Mass at the church of Our Lady of Lourdes, his coffin, draped with a Union Jack together with his fireman's helmet, axe and bandsman's cap, was carried by colleagues from the Brigade Messrs Bodger, West, Finch, Pearce, Harvey and Horan, while the hearse was driven by Fireman Burrows. It seemed that almost the entire community had turned out to pay its respects and witness the funeral procession as it proceeded up Lawn Road and along the High Street to beyond The Greenway. Traffic came to a standstill as the long cortege slow marched past the crowd lining the High Street. It was headed by a body of the Metropolitan Police, followed by over fifty firemen in full dress uniform including Chief Officer Harry Gales and Hon. Sec. G.J. Crook. Then came the Silver Band led by Mr A.B. Sims, playing my grandfather's favourite hymn 'Days and Moments' and the 'Dead March' from 'Saul'. Following the band were members of the RAF Central Band, representatives of twenty neighbouring brigades, local dignitaries Alderman H.S. Button JP, Maj. R.W.C. Flavell JP, Mr R.W. Hudson JP and others, close friends including Messrs Bell, Finch, Gardiner, Sopp, Worley and Brown, and finally the hearse and family mourners' cars. At the municipal offices the flag flew at half mast, and council officers stood to attention as the procession passed in what was a fitting tribute to a greatly respected member of the community. Being so young I was spared a lot of the grieving, although I don't think my grandmother or mother ever really got over the shock.

I did not know him for long, but later I gathered that I was the apple of his eye. This probably accounts for the inscription on my parents' second wreath, 'His best boy, to Grandpa'.

My elementary school, St Mary's, in Rockingham Road.

Two years later, on 12 June 1933, my schooldays began at St Mary's, Rockingham Road – a small, Victorian brick and slate building with only three classrooms, each with an open fireplace. The school roll numbered about 100, and the teaching staff comprised the head, Elizabeth Hoey, and sisters Molly and Madge Smith – a formidable trio who collectively chalked up over 100 years of service.

We were fed a strict diet of the three R's and the headmistress, a strong disciplinarian and brilliant academic, also displayed her generosity by treating us to a seaside outing every summer in addition to educational cinema visits.

Molly Smith not only included maths, English, history, geography and nature study in her repertoire, but also taught needlework, country dancing and physical training. Additionally she ran the girls' netball team, and because of a great interest in soccer originating from her Geordie background, the boys' football team as well. All this on a salary of £195 per annum. After she died in 1996, I felt honoured when her family invited me to deliver the eulogy at her funeral service.

During the 1930s, the majority of pupils walked to school. Some had a bus or train journey as well. Bicycles were a luxury few could afford. Those who lived nearby, as I did, went home to lunch; the rest brought sandwiches. No canteens in those days! A ha'penny bottle of milk – a third of a pint – was available during the morning break, when the playgrounds became hives of activity. Boys and girls were separated by a wire fence and no one dared to cross the frontier.

The boys' main pastime was football played with a tennis ball but non-players found numerous other interests. 'Fag' cards, marbles, 'five-stones', conkers, 'bung the barrel' were all in evidence while a thriving trade existed in swapping anything from cigarette cards to 'tuppenny bloods' such as *Hotspur, Wizard, Adventure* and *Rover* comics.

On the road to school, by Rockingham Bridge, stood a small, shack-like, corrugated-iron sweetshop called The Bon Bon. Owned by Charles and Avis Rashbrook who lived nearby, it housed a treasure chest of goodies displayed invitingly under its glass counter top. A ha'penny

Avis Rashbrook in the doorway of 'The Bon Bon', her sweet shop by Rockingham Bridge.

could purchase a sherbet fountain, liquorice pipe or bootlaces, 'everlasting strip' toffee, aniseed balls or gobstoppers – and prices started at a farthing. Only the poorest children – and unfortunately there were several – could pass the shop without buying something.

Two months after I started at St Mary's, a new teacher joined the staff of Frays College, the private school in Harefield Road. He was Eric Blair, who would achieve fame later through his books *Animal Farm* and 1984, written under his pseudonym George Orwell. Mr Orwell was one of a number of distinguished residents of Uxbridge over the years. Anti-slave campaigner William Wilberforce lived at Chestnut House, Honeycroft Hill from 1824-1826, the renowned Victorian actress Ellen Terry used a medieval house at the western end of the High Street as a weekend cottage during the 1880s, and T.E. Lawerence, better known as Lawrence of Arabia, was a recruit at RAF Uxbridge in 1922, using an alias – John Hume Ross. His book *The Mint* chronicles his stay at Uxbridge. In addition, stage and film actor Bernard Miles was born and bred in Hillingdon.

George Orwell left Frays College after only one term due to catching pneumonia and spending time in Uxbridge Cottage Hospital during January 1934. Soon afterwards I had my first introduction to that same hospital when our family doctor Harold Vickers referred me for an exploratory throat examination followed by a second one at Guy's Hospital in London. The results of both proved inconclusive – the consultant at Guy's only succeeding in knocking out my front teeth!

During the 1930s, many tradesmen provided a home delivery service. Consequently, our road was often busy with milk floats, bakers' and greengrocers' vans. The Uxbridge Sanitary Laundry van made a weekly collection and delivery of washing. Cycles, too, played their part, used by 'Sooty' Wilson the sweep from Cowley Road, George Osborne who worked for Nicholls the pork butcher, Bill Kelly from Palmer's Ironmongers who occasionally stopped for a quick game of football or cricket in Rockingham Recreation Ground in between rounds, and the lamplighter who could be seen from our window igniting the gas lamp opposite, without

A ward in the Uxbridge Cottage Hospital, Harefield Road.

dismounting from his cycle. Albert Marlow, the window cleaner from Chapel Street pushed his ladders and buckets on a barrow, and smartly uniformed postmen delivered parcels from a large, red, wicker barrow, in addition to letter deliveries three times a day. The Walls Ice Cream 'Stop Me & Buy One' tricycle was always popular, as was the alternative – the Eldorado man. Another welcome visitor was the Muffin Man (on foot), who announced his arrival by ringing a handbell while balancing a tray of his wares on his head. The horse-drawn dustcart came weekly, driven by a man called 'Moulder', obviously a nickname, and when his son joined him on the round, he inevitably became known as 'Young Moulder.' Coal carts and horses were a regular sight in winter, the coalmen wearing sacks shaped like cowls on their heads, giving them a monk-like appearance, albeit with coal-black faces, and another horse and cart trader was the rag and bone man with his familiar cry of 'Rag-bone'.

We were certainly spoilt for choice in those days, as apart from all the delivery services, there were twenty-eight shops all within five minutes walk away! The one we used most was Staniford's in Cowley Road – a newsagent and confectioner run with expert efficiency by Edith Weinberger, known to everyone as 'Edie.' Next door was Keyworth's bakers, who would sell us a whole bag of 'yesterday's cakes' for 1d or 2d, and another favourite at 39 Windsor Street was the small sweet shop established by Albert Webb and his wife in 1933. After her parents' death, the business was carried on by their daughter Margaret Walbridge until 2001. The street, which dates from the thirteenth century, was the location of several interesting shops, including Edwards and Simmonds (cooked meats), James Pond's bakery and Jack Hutton's fish shop – a new venture for the entrepreneur who had opened the town's first cinema, Rockingham Hall, in 1910.

Yet for me, the jewel in the Windsor Street crown was undoubtedly Hannah Baldwin's tiny toyshop, truly an Aladdin's cave – and almost as dark inside. It was a treasure trove of every kind of toy, with prices starting at ½d and 1d. Just to look around was exciting, as every bit of space was crammed full of goodies such as catapults, pea-shooters, cap pistols, toy soldiers, farm

Our local newsagent and confectioner, Staniford's in Cowley Road. On the left is Plested's, Coach & Motor Body Builders.

Our nearest baker's, Keyworth's, next to another Staniford shop, a draper's.

Albert Webb's sweet shop at 39 Windsor Street.

Proprietor Albert Webb behind the counter of the shop he opened in 1933.

Albert's daughter Margaret Walbridge, who took over the running of the business after her parents' death.

animals, model cars, fishing nets and, in November, Guy Fawkes masks, to name a few. One item, however, which struck a sour note with children, was a bunch of canes – the type used in schools at that time!

Apart from the shopkeepers, hundreds of tradesmen were employed by the South Uxbridge factories including the Bell Punch, Steel Barrels, Metesco Electric Co., and the Gas and Water companies. 'Clocking off' time was usually 5.30 p.m. (you could set your watch by their works' hooters) and for the next half-hour long crocodiles of workmen threaded their way along Rockingham Road and Recreation Ground into the town to catch buses or trains. They formed an integral part of Uxbridge's industrial history.

Nearly all our leisure time was spent out in the open air. Being so close at hand, the Rockingham and Fassnidge parks were the most frequented places of amusement. Further afield, there were, however, many popular locations; Swakeleys woods where we climbed trees, made camps and picked blackberries, the Frayswater, generally known as 'the floodgates', where woodland and riverbank ran parallel with the branch railway line from Uxbridge High Street railway station to Denham, the Common, ideal for picnics, ball games and sailing toy boats on the pond, and Fountain's Meadows which stretched from the Grand Union canal to the back end of Denham Village. The meadows were bordered on one side by the River Colne and its suspension bridge and on the other by a shallow tributary that was perfect for paddling. Another stretch of the Colne flowing under Long Bridge on Uxbridge Moor was a favourite venue for youngsters who fished for tiddlers, armed with a penny fishing net and a jam jar. The adjacent meadow was the site of the popular Beach's Fair whose annual visit was eagerly awaited.

The RAF Camp was another provider of several sources of recreation. On summer evenings, I and a schoolmate, whose parents lived in the married quarters, spent many hours exploring

The start of Windsor Street, where we did much of our shopping.

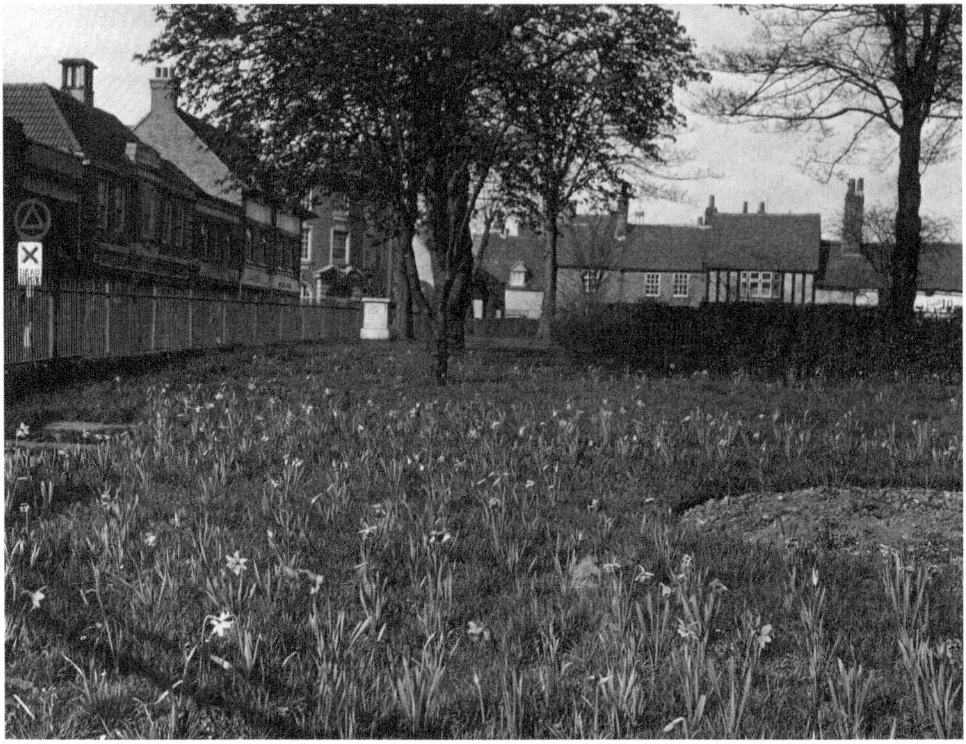

- DEWHURST -
34 STANIFORD 34
LANGSTON & CO LTD
J. H. Dewhurst Ltd
NEWSAGENT
MAGAZINES

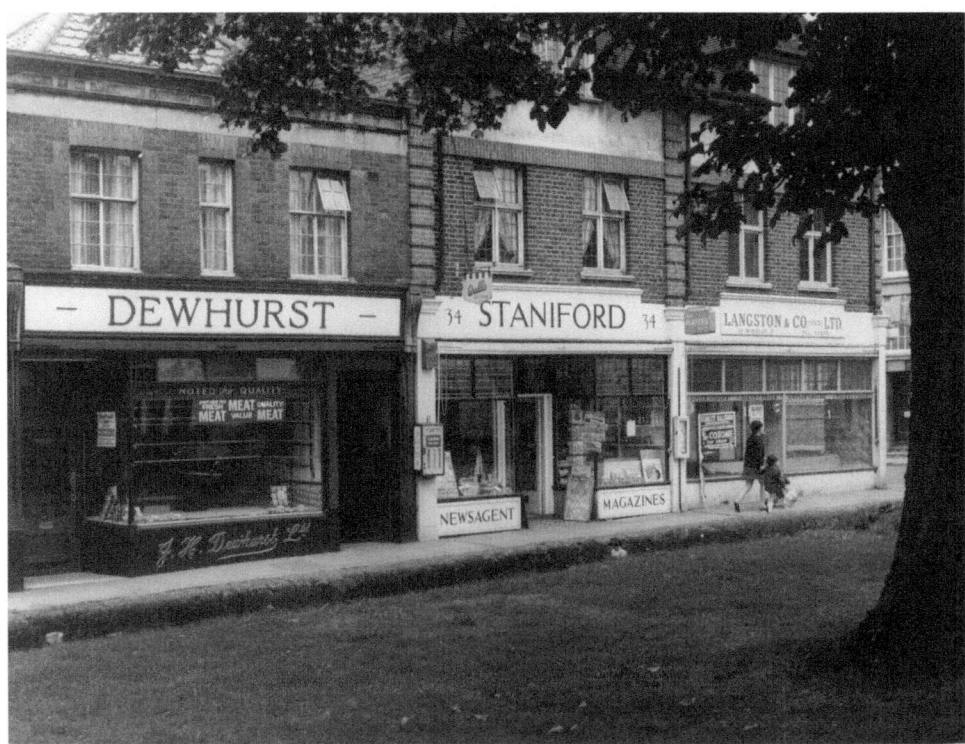

Opposite above: An attractive view of the Old Burial Ground opposite the shops, especially when the daffodils were coming into bloom.

Opposite below: A later picture of Windsor Street. The railings around the Burial Ground have been removed – not for the war effort – but to improve drivers' sightlines.

Right: Fassnidge Memorial Park, commonly known as the 'Swing Rec'. Not interested in the swings on this occasion, my sister Diana proudly displays her new doll's pram.

Below: This part of the River Frays served as a makeshift bathing pool before Uxbridge Swimming Pool opened in 1935.

The High Street railway station overlooking the River Frays near the 'floodgates'. Passenger services ended on 31 August 1939, although goods traffic continued until January 1964.

Uxbridge Common with the familiar landmark of the water tower on the skyline.

what was, to us, an adventure playground. With the narrow River Pinn, or Pinn Brook as it was sometimes known, meandering through the wooded glades of wild flowers and the incessant cawing of rooks in the tall trees, it resembled a country park rather than an Air Force barracks. The camp was open to the general public until the outbreak of the Second World War, and the route from the St Andrews Gate off the High Street to the Vine Lane, Hillingdon exit, provided a popular walk for local residents.

Since 1923, the camp had been the home of Uxbridge Football Club, one of the oldest amateur teams in the country. Since its foundation in 1871, the club led a nomadic existence playing on fifteen different home grounds, but now enjoyed the luxury of a new stadium – at least until 1939. I watched many of Uxbridge's home games during the late 1930s, some from the height of a giant scoreboard used for athletics meetings staged on the perimeter running track. The club also had the use of the RAF Depot Ground bordering the Hillingdon Road for midweek evening matches.

Another entertainment facility offered by the camp was its cinema which began life in 1919 as a lecture hall, gymnasium and cinema for RAF personnel only. Eventually it opened its doors to the general public, and we enjoyed several visits until its enforced closure on 2 September, 1939. The films screened there were second or third time around and the seating very basic on a non-sloping concrete floor, but with a child's admission price of 3d, we weren't complaining.

At the other end of the spectrum, the Regal Cinema which had opened on Boxing Day 1931 was positively luxurious by comparison. It was built on Park Lodge Estate, which was said to include the largest oak tree in Middlesex, and was completed in twenty-two weeks by an army of 350 workmen. One of these was Ralph Rumble, who told me that he worked a seventy-seven-hour week from Sunday to Saturday for an hourly wage of 1s 7d. He considered himself fortunate to have a job at the height of the Depression.

Uxbridge Football Club at the RAF Stadium ground.

The RAF camp cinema with replica bombs on either side of the entrance.

The sumptuous grandeur of the Regal cinema auditorium shows why it is still a Grade II★ Listed building. As regular attenders of its Saturday-morning pictures, we were known as 'Union Chums.'

The Regal, which attracted 750,000 customers during its first year of operation, became a regular source of entertainment for us during the late 1930s. It was here that we attended the Saturday morning children's shows known for obvious reasons as the 'tuppenny rush'. The programme consisted of a cartoon and a sixty minute 'B Western', while sandwiched in between was a ten-minute chapter of a twelve-part serial. Each episode ended with a cliffhanger situation to entice us back on the following Saturday. All week long, we speculated as to whether or not the hero would escape from his desperate plight. Of course, he always did! Another item featured in the programme was community singing, accompanied by the Compton organ. To make it easy for us, the words of popular favourites like 'Red Sails In The Sunset', 'Roll Along Covered Wagon' and 'South Of The Border' were projected on to the screen.

During the cricket season I spent most weekends at the Uxbridge Cricket Club ground in Cricket Field Road, which had opened in 1858. After a while I was allowed to sit behind the scorers on the balcony at one end of the old thatched pavilion and hang up the numbers on the scoreboard. Living so near, I was able to go home for tea during the interval and be back in time for the restart. At other times I took sandwiches and a bottle of Tizer, and made a day of it. When Uxbridge were playing away, I watched the Bell Punch works team at their ground (The Island) and performed the same task of putting up their scores.

The weather seemed to be kinder to us for watching and playing sport in those days. At least the seasons were as regular as clockwork – well almost. They were both predictable and consistent. Keats and Shakespeare got it right when they wrote about a 'season of mists and mellow fruitfulness' (Keats, *To Autumn*), or 'when icicles hang by the wall' (Shakespeare, *Loves Labour's Lost*). Songwriters too, were spot on with their lyrics. After the winds of March, April showers came in right on cue along with the first cuckoo, and May blossom actually bloomed

A glimpse of the Regal's narrow (15yd-long) frontage, a year after its opening. Two years later, one of our favourite toy shops, Percy's, was built next to the shoe shop.

The narrow entrance to Cricketfield Road, off Vine Street.

A weekend match in progress at the Uxbridge CC ground.

Horse and rider in perfect unison at the Uxbridge Show on August Bank Holiday 1936. For once it was not raining.

A typical wintry scene at the entrance to Willowbank Estate, Denham. Old Mill House stands on the left, and Denham Lodge is on the right.

in May. Flaming June lived up to its name and July usually featured a thunderstorm or two. On occasion, it rained during the August Bank Holiday weekend (the date of the annual Uxbridge Show), and sure enough 'the leaves of brown came tumbling down' in September. October winds were followed by the inevitable fogs in November – many of them being the proverbial 'pea-soupers', while December and January automatically brought snow and a white Christmas.

At a time when a great part of the world map was coloured in pink – denoting the British Empire, on which it was said 'the sun never sets', there was a great sense of national pride, and nowhere more so than in our schools. On Empire Day (24 May) we paraded in the playground, unashamedly singing patriotic songs, marching and flag-waving. Pupils were encouraged to bring union flags to school and many houses flew them from their windows. The afternoon was always a school holiday. Additionally we commemorated St George's, St Andrew's, St David's and St Patrick's days in their turn.

Another traditional annual event always celebrated in great style was Guy Fawkes' night on 5 November. I well remember peering out of our front-room window through the gathering gloom, watching for my father to arrive home from work – particularly to see if he was clutching a parcel under his arm. If so, it meant we were having a firework display after tea. Rarely were we disappointed.

A big occasion for national celebration was King George V's and Queen Mary's Silver Jubilee on 6 May 1935. We enjoyed a three-day holiday from school, a cinema show and tea party. Uxbridge staged one of the most spectacular carnivals in its history. The Jubilee parade processed through the town led by a lone mounted hussar followed by hundreds of floats and cars representing every local organisation. The carnival king and queen, James Dean and Muriel Robbins, pupils of Swakeleys School, rode in a carriage drawn by six magnificent horses, with four outriders. The day ended with a torchlight procession led by the RAF, followed by a massive fireworks display and bonfire on the common.

A somewhat lesser event, but of great importance to the town, was the opening of Uxbridge Swimming Pool on 31 August 1935. Important because, prior to that date, the only swimming facility was a murky, somewhat suspect section of the River Frays where it flowed parallel to Harefield Road. The opening ceremony was performed by the chairman of the council, Reverend Luther Bouch, and the first superintendent was Alf Price, who in 1952 would manage the British Olympic squad. The new pool soon attracted 4,000 customers a day.

A few days earlier, on 27 August, a new wing was opened at St Mary's, comprising three classrooms, cloakrooms and a staff room. The total cost, including a more modern heating system, amounted to £4,000, and the building work was completed in two months. A school building fund was established, with pupils asked to contribute 1d per week, and a collection was taken up every Monday morning.

A penny a week may seem trivial by today's standards, but in the 1930s its spending power was quite remarkable, especially when considering that the current 1p coin is worth 2½ times the value of its predecessor. An old penny could buy a large broadsheet newspaper and children's comic, a postage stamp that ensured a next day delivery, a bread roll or currant bun, and numerous confectionery items. Some popular favourites were a pennyworth of chips from the fish shop and a pennyworth of broken chocolate from Woolworths, not forgetting a penny Walls snowfrute or a packet of tablets that made eight glasses of fizzy lemonade.

We used pennies in our gas meter, collected 'pennies for the guy' in readiness for Guy Fawkes night, 'spent a penny' in public conveniences, bought a 'penny on the ball' raffle ticket for a new football at Uxbridge's home matches, and were rewarded with a 'Saturday penny' from our parents if we had behaved ourselves. Many of our toys costing only 1d included fishing nets, pea-shooters, cap-pistols and toy soldiers made from real lead – no plastic in those days!

Adults who had several pennies to spend – plus a few pounds – could purchase a new three-bedroom semi for around £350-400, an Austin 7 car for £120; and hire an electric cooker for 6d per week.

We'd never had it so good!

Within months of his Silver Jubilee, King George V died on 20 January 1936, and I have a vivid memory of the newspaper placards outside Staniford's announcing 'The King Is Dead' in funereal purple print. When George's eldest son was proclaimed King Edward VIII, all local schoolchildren received a commemorative beaker in advance of his coronation. Unfortunately this became a coronation that never was, as on 10 December he renounced the throne and abdicated. His brother Albert replaced him, deciding to use the name George VI, and was crowned King on 12 May 1937. So now we were presented with another coronation mug, a souvenir medal and a book, entitled 'The Crowning of the King and Queen'. This was followed by a tea party at St John's Hall on Uxbridge Moor, with the icing on the cake being a week's holiday from school.

Once again Uxbridge celebrated the event in great style with a procession around the town which included the Uxbridge and Hillingdon Prize Band, the Dagenham Girl Pipers and Carnival Queen Joan Price. She was attended by her six maids of honour, Irene Harris, Edith Lowe, Peggy Foster, Ivy Kilbey and Misses M. Searle and D. Cooper. As usual on these occasions, the celebrations culminated with a firework display and bonfire on the common. A film made of the day's events was screened at the Regal Cinema the following week.

Meanwhile, back in 1936, major developments were taking place a couple of miles away from the town which were to have a significant effect on the future of the British film industry. Work had begun in 1935 on a vast film studio at Denham, the brainchild of Sir Alexander Korda. By February 1936, film production was up and running, even before all the building work had been completed. Then, on 30 September 1936, a sister studio was opened at Pinewood, two miles from Uxbridge, in the opposite direction. Eventually the two studios amalgamated under the title D & P Studios, and because of its close proximity to both buildings, the town soon became a much-used location for film making.

Another welcome event closer to home was the advent of the trolleybus, replacing the electric tramcar service that dated from May 1904. The first trial run took place on 9 November 1936, and I had the pleasure of riding on the smooth streamlined 607, on its first day of public service, Sunday 15 November. The almost noiseless trolleybus was a complete contrast to the rumbling, clanging tram – uncomfortable and prone to breaking down. At school on the Monday following, we were required to write an essay (called a composition in those days) on the arrival of this new mode of transport, and I remember describing it departing from the newly built terminus at the western end of the High Street 'gliding gracefully as a swan'. Waxing lyrical, I suppose, but I was very impressed.

1938 would prove to be a momentous year for the nation as a whole, but also saw many memorable local events. In February, a tragic accident occurred when a Hawker Hurricane piloted by an Uxbridge man nose-dived into the edge of Swakeley's woods close to the Western Avenue (now the A40). I was one of many who visited the scene after the aircraft's removal and shall never forget the image of the deep chasm of rich brown clay caused by the crash. Was it a sign of things to come?

On a lighter note, there were plenty of ongoing happy events for our amusement. One of our school's benefactresses was Mrs Gilbey who lived at 'The Lea' in Denham. She held an annual garden party to which the staff and pupils were invited, and provided a horse-drawn brake which transported us from the Oxford Road down the long drive to the grounds of her estate. In return, the children performed country dancing for the spectators. Other happy occasions

The High Street procession to commemorate King George V's and Queen Mary's Silver Jubilee in 1935.

A full house attending the opening of Uxbridge Swimming Pool, an open-air pool with icy-cold water!

The pool on a much quieter day.

Opposite above: Jack Hutton's second fish shop in Vine Street. Conveniently situated next to the entrance to the Burial Ground, where we could sit in comfort while eating our penny bags of chips.

Opposite below: One of the most popular High Street shops was Woolworth's 3d and 6d stores (right of centre) where 1d could buy a bag of broken chocolate or biscuits, and a lot more besides.

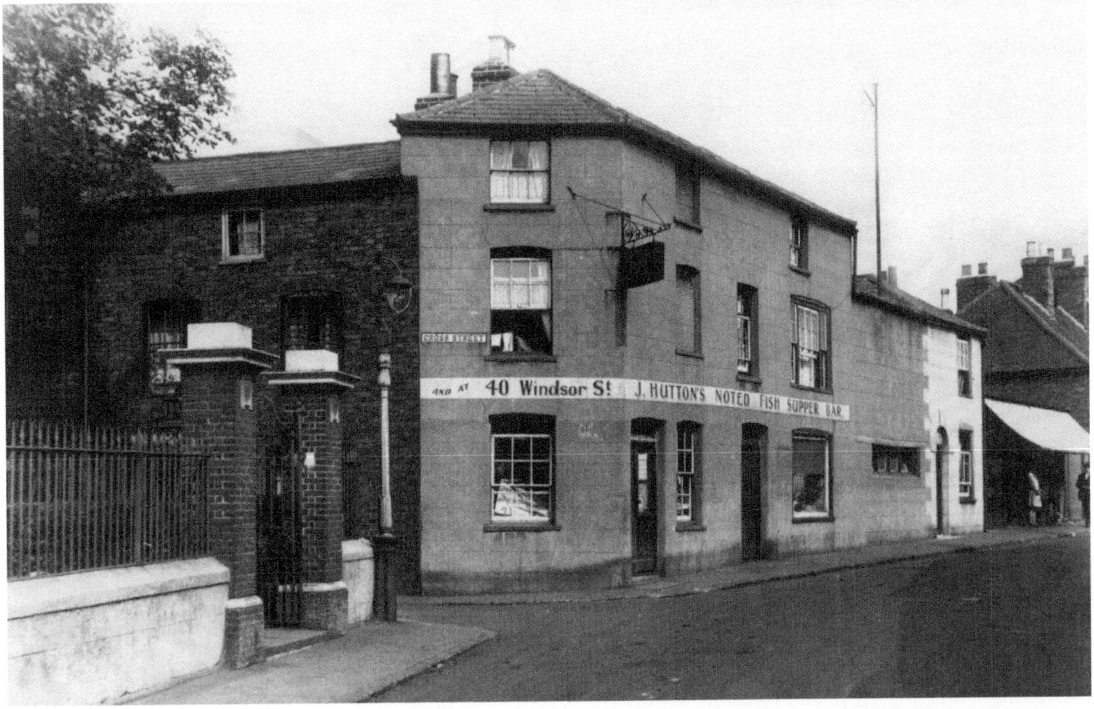
AND AT 40 Windsor St
J. HUTTON'S NOTED FISH SUPPER BAR.

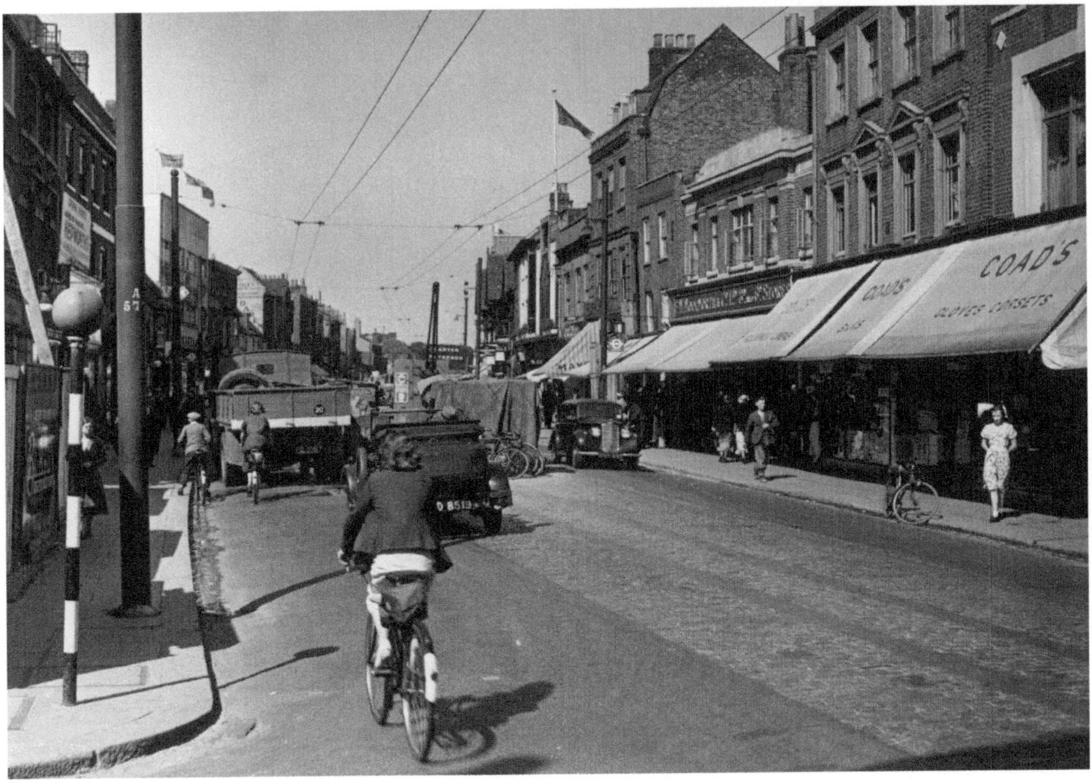
COAD'S
GLOVES CORSETS
COAD'S

The ever popular Walls Ice Cream tricycle has stopped in Wilmar Close to the delight of local residents. Left to right: Ken Pearce (future local historian), Bobby Dell, Donald Burton, Harold Newby, Esther Newby, Ian Bray, Beryl Gorman, Rosalie Pearce, David Smith. The Walls man would call at any house displaying a card bearing a large 'W' in the window.

Frank Cooper's bakery and tea rooms (left of picture) was the first High Street shop I remember. My mother took me there regularly in my pram to buy delicious sponge fingers.

The Uxbridge Electric Supply Co. (on the right), hired out cookers for 6d per week, and a 3pt electric kettle came free with them. The Chain Library (on the left) charged a 2d lending fee, and their windows always displayed *William* books in colourful dust jackets, which I read avidly.

Of most interest to me in this High Street parade of shops was Curry's, who stocked toys as well as electrical goods and cycles. A treasured birthday present bought there was a green scooter, price 5s.

Cover of the Souvenir Brochure for Coronation Day, 1937.

MONDAY MAY 17th

The "Middlesex Advertiser and County Gazette"

IN CONJUNCTION WITH

UNION CINEMAS LTD.

WILL PRESENT AT THE

UNION CINEMA'S REGAL UXBRIDGE

THREE TIMES DAILY FOR THE WHOLE WEEK

UXBRIDGE CORONATION SOUND FILM REVIEW

SHOWING HOW UXBRIDGE CELEBRATED THE CORONATION OF H.M. KING GEORGE VI.

AND ALSO THIS FILM WILL BE SHOWN THE FOLLOWING WEEK AT THE

UNION CINEMA'S MARLBORO' YIEWSLEY

THIS FILM, AFTER ITS SHOWING WILL BE PRESENTED, IN A GOLDEN CASKET, TO THE TOWN AS A SOUVENIR OF THE CORONATION OF MAY 12th, 1937.

Newspaper advertisement for the Coronation film.

The Market House and shops dressed up in red, white and blue for the occasion.

St John's Road, Uxbridge Moor, where local schools enjoyed a Coronation tea party at the church hall.

Denham Film Studios, shortly after completion.

New trolleybuses waiting to leave their High Street terminus.

40

included Sunday evening band concerts in Fassnidge Park, and the regular visits of the fair and circus to the Swan and Bottle and Dog and Duck meadows.

The most exciting of all, however, came on 19 March, when I saw my first professional football match. Our teacher, Molly Smith, took a school party to Griffin Park, where Brentford lost to Liverpool 1-3. Then, on Easter Monday, 18 April, I accompanied my father to the same ground and saw Brentford defeat league leaders Arsenal 3-0. These were the days when top footballers earned £7-8 per week, plus a win bonus of £2 and £1 for a draw. On that Monday, for the London derby, the crowd totalled 38,000 – the ground's capacity at the time. A regular custom then, before the days of stringent safety regulations, was for small boys to be passed over the heads of spectators from the top rows of the terraces right down to the edge of the pitch, to enable them to see the game. Quite a novel experience for me – a little frightening, in fact, and I did not see my father again until after the match.

Throughout the decade, the town had witnessed many improvements to benefit the community, in particular the large-scale slum clearances in the yards north of the High Street, and the creation of several council housing estates. There were improvements to schools and highways, and plans were in place for the building of new municipal offices to include a clinic, library and museum.

In June 1938, Uxbridge had a new luxury cinema, the Odeon, which seated 1,837 patrons. An old hotel, the Brookfield, and an adjoining house, Hurstlea, at the western end of the High Street were demolished a year earlier, and the site left unattended while waiting for building work to start. Some friends and I took advantage of this, finding it a great place to explore the underground passages and cellars of the old buildings. The official opening on 20 June was one of glitzy razzamatazz, as the stars of the opening film *The Drum*, Sabu and Valerie Hobson made

Molly Smith with her 'class of 37' in the playground of St Mary's (the author is in the bottom right corner).

Sir Alexander Korda showing a reel of film from *The Drum* to Prime Minister Neville Chamberlain during his visit to Denham Studios, not long before his momentous trip to Munich.

Uxbridge's largest and most modern cinema, the Odean. The entrance to the wartime Food Office is seen on the left.

personal appearances along with Anna Neagle and husband Herbert Wilcox. Also in attendance was the RAF Central Band and pipers of the King's Own Scottish Borderers, and the event was given considerable coverage by the *Gaumont British News* – screened at the cinema during the following week.

Sabu was an Indian orphan brought back to England after making the film *Elephant Boy*, and installed in a private boarding school in nearby Beaconsfield. Mad about football, he played for the school team Beaconsfield Rovers, and occasionally for the town team as well. With his salary going into a trust fund, he was allowed only 1s a week for pocket money. Nevertheless, he owned a silver, open-top sports car and was often seen driving through Uxbridge on his way to a London gymnasium or to Earls Court Rink to pursue his second hobby – ice skating.

Six months after the Odeon opening came another welcome addition to the town and another excellent example of 1930s architecture in the form of the new Underground station built in a central point of the High Street, replacing the 1904 terminus in Belmont Road. It opened on 4 December 1938.

Sabu, Indian born star of *Elephant Boy*, *The Drum* and *The Thief of Baghdad* could often be seen around Uxbridge, and sometimes having tea in Cooper's tea rooms.

Above: Demolition work in progress on shops facing the Market House to prepare the way for the new Underground station.

Opposite: The impressive finished article – one of the last examples of 1930s architecture in the town.

However, while Uxbridge was progressing steadily towards a kind of urban Utopia, conditions around the globe were fast deteriorating. There were wars and rumours of wars – China versus Japan, the Spanish Civil War and the Jewish-Arab conflict. Inevitably, most British eyes were focused on Europe, and in particular on Adolf Hitler's Germany. It was against this background that the country began preparing for the awesome prospect of being involved in a second war within twenty years.

A government order made in January 1938 stipulated that all children be issued with gas masks, and, along with other schools in the district, 175 of us at St Mary's received ours in September. We were instructed on how to wear them, and subsequently had to pass through a 'gas van' to test them. Later that month a load of sand was delivered to the school, followed by a set of Air Raid Precautions (ARP) equipment consisting of one sand bucket and a combined shovel/scoop. Shades of *Dad's Army*!

Earlier, in June, an ARP service had been set up in a large house in the High Street, and volunteer workers were recruited in addition to auxiliary firemen. However, on 30 September, the nation breathed a huge sigh of relief as we received some joyous news. At 5.40 p.m. the Prime Minister, Neville Chamberlain, alighted from his aeroplane at the tiny Heston aerodrome, a few miles from Uxbridge. In his hand was a piece of paper bearing two signatures – his own and that of Adolf Hitler. It was the Anglo-German 'no war' agreement signed a few hours earlier at Munich. From Heston, where thousands of people had greeted him with a tumultuous reception, Mr Chamberlain was driven to Buckingham Palace, where another 10,000 well-wishers were waiting in pouring rain. Then at 7.00 p.m., he appeared on the Palace balcony with his wife and the King and Queen, caught in the beam of a giant searchlight. The crowd's welcome was described the following day in the *Daily Herald* as 'frenzied'. Later, at Downing

Street, he spoke from an upstairs window and uttered those oft quoted words, 'I believe it is peace for our time'.

Unfortunately it was not. The wording on the document that the Premier had held aloft to his delirious admirers clearly was not worth the paper it was written on.

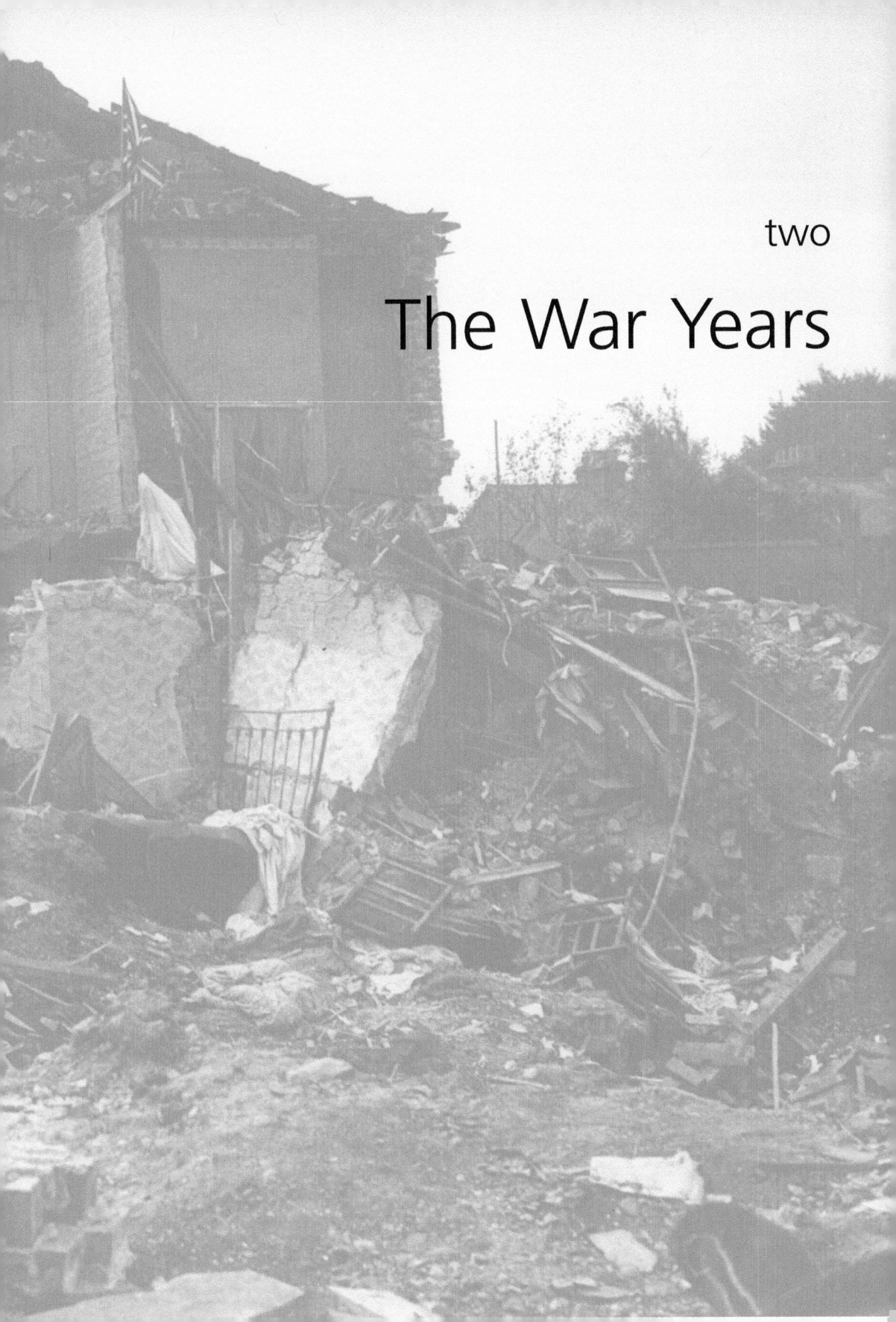

two
The War Years

As we entered the last year of the decade, the emergency measures started in 1938 began to gather momentum. The elation of that previous September evening was evaporating as more and more people sensed that Mr Chamberlain's appeasement policy was not going to halt the Nazis' progress through Europe, nor deter them from their ultimate aim of world domination.

The Prime Minister had met with opposition from his own party as far back as February 1938 when foreign secretary Anthony Eden resigned because of their differences of opinion. In addition, several of Chamberlain's colleagues were highly critical of his policies – none more so than his eventual successor, Winston Churchill.

Even leaving aside the Parliamentary wrangling – and there was plenty – the Britain of 1939 was not a happy one. That old *bête noir*, unemployment, had soared to 1.9 million, and, as time went on, war clouds were looming ominously on the horizon. Certainly the preparations being made now had a really serious look about them.

Throughout the country, Anderson corrugated-iron air-raid shelters were being delivered to individual houses, free to householders earning less than £5 a week and costing £7 for everyone else. Workmen were digging up parks and open spaces to create underground shelters, while brick-built overground shelters were erected as alternatives.

Trenches being dug for air-raid shelters on land opposite the Common – now the home of Uxbridge Cricket Club.

The surface air-raid shelter in Rockingham Recreation Ground, similar to those in many of our streets.

In Uxbridge the first of these were sited in Laundry Yard and Cricketfield Road followed by many others in residential areas. We had one in How's Close and another in nearby Rockingham Recreation Ground. Further new developments in the town included the formation of a second TA (Territorial Army) unit in addition to the existing 'D' Company, 8th Battalion Middlesex Regiment based at the Whitehall Road Drill Hall. The new unit's headquarters were in Cowley High Street, where it was attached to the 75th Searchlight Regiment, Royal Artillery. Then air-raid sirens were installed and tested, while forty-four ARP wardens' posts were set up in and around Uxbridge.

Meanwhile, the government announced plans to introduce conscription, double the strength of the Territorials, and evacuate 2.5 million children from possible danger areas. The RAF was being equipped with over 400 new aircraft a month.

All of this activity passed over the heads of us, the younger generation, as we remained oblivious and blissfully unaware of the dangers that lay ahead. I cannot remember our parents discussing the prospect of war, and in any event, when not indulging in sport and other leisure activities, I was preparing for my forthcoming school exams – the 'scholarship' – later known as the eleven plus. When the big day arrived, I was fortunate enough to pass and gain a place at Gunnersbury Grammar School, just outside London. I left my junior school on 26 July in the middle of a long hot summer, looking forward to the new experience of starting grammar school in September.

But things did not work out that way.

Just four hours after Hitler's army invaded Poland on the morning of Friday 1 September, a hired Daimler driven by Bert Burrows in full chauffeur's uniform drew up outside our house. Bert's father, Albert, had established a carrier's and undertaker's business in the early 1900s, and his premises were round the corner from us in Cowley Road. My father was a family friend.

My sister, two brothers and I had no idea what was happening as we were marshalled into the car by my mother and next door neighbour Evelyn Palmer, wife of the Windsor Street ironmonger. When we asked questions, my mother said we were going on a surprise holiday. Eventually we arrived at a small village called New Mill near the market town of Tring in Hertfordshire. What we didn't know was that we were part of a mass evacuation programme involving one million children on that same morning. Only we were luckier, having our mother with us and the luxury of a private car. The others were herded into trains like lost lambs with name tags around their necks and gas masks over their shoulders. Mrs Palmer had kindly arranged for us to stay with her parents when it seemed that war was imminent. We were made welcome immediately and that night at supper (bread, cheese and pickled onions) our host Mr Richards produced a bottle of Tizer, having heard that it was our favourite drink.

On returning to the house from church on Sunday morning, we sensed an air of foreboding. Mr and Mrs Richards were sitting grim faced listening to the wireless. It was 11.15, and in a strained, sombre voice, Neville Chamberlain was announcing that 'This country is now at war with Germany'. Almost immediately the sirens sounded – the first of many false alarms. That afternoon, our host took us to a nearby beauty spot and as we strolled round a huge lake, there was an eerie stillness over the whole area. I shall never forget the airless, humid atmosphere as we passed fishermen by the lakeside and families out walking. It could have been any ordinary Sunday afternoon. Unfortunately, it was not.

During the week that followed, I became homesick and slightly depressed. When my father, who had remained at home because of his job, came to visit us at the weekend, I persuaded my parents to allow me to return to Uxbridge with him. My new school had been evacuated to Chesham, Bucks, and my starting date postponed which meant an extended summer holiday. I was a free agent, relishing an unexpected spell of freedom. I did not realise that it would be my last holiday in peacetime for six years.

My former elementary school St Mary's had remained closed, along with all others, since the outbreak of war. It was allowed to reopen on 17 October under certain conditions. No more than sixty pupils could attend at one time and no child under seven could be included. The outcome was that two groups of sixty received two hours of schooling per day, although eventually the time was extended. Another regulation was that all staff and pupils must keep their gas masks with them at all times. In fact, we were all constantly reminded to do this, and at one stage early in the war, cinemas threatened to refuse admission to anyone not carrying a respirator. Children did not always treat their masks with respect. Boys discovered that they could produce rude noises by exhaling sharply after fitting them on and some used the cardboard containers for collecting pieces of shrapnel after the blitz began in 1940.

The area had become a bustling hive of activity since the declaration of war. The building of air-raid shelters started in 1938 was stepped up, especially in the schools. Squads of Territorials and occasionally the regular army were marching through the streets and drilling in recreation grounds. Civil defence wardens' posts were much in evidence, there was extra activity at Vine Street Fire Station and the new Auxiliary Fire Service (AFS) post in The Lynch, and men were 'digging for victory' on allotments and anywhere else that was available.

In common with the schools, all the cinemas were closed by government order, but after a fortnight it was back to 'business as usual'. Throughout the 1930s, cinema had become a great trendsetter, influencing all our lives. Fashions, make-up, smoking and American slang were all copied from the movies. And the younger generation re-enacted the cowboy and adventure stories. Now, more than ever, the film had an even more important part to play, not only as a morale boosting form of escapism, but also as a powerful propaganda weapon. It soon became the nation's No. 1 form of entertainment, with over 25 million going to the pictures every week

Uxbridge AFS engaged in a practice exercise outside the Bell Punch Co. by the 'Dolphin' Bridge.

Their West Drayton counterparts doing likewise by the canalside near Yiewsley Bridge.

Uxbridge AFS men at their headquarters, the former St Margaret's School in The Lynch.

Yiewsley Town Hall, well protected by sandbags at the outbreak of war, 1939.

The Duke of Kent opening the new youth centre adjacent to Rockingham Recreation Ground on 11 March 1939. Sharing the platform left to right: W.G. Pomeroy, John Poole, Harold Leno, John Miles, W.S. Try (on the Duke's left).

Prior to the opening the Duke inspected the 100-strong Uxbridge Air Defence Cadets, the first squadron to provide a guard of honour for any member of the Royal Family. The Duke, who lived nearby at Iver, was killed in an air crash on 24 August 1942.

Left: June Duprez, star of *The Four Feathers* and *The Thief of Baghdad*, was due to make a personal appearance at the Odeon on 4 September 1939, but the war put paid to that. She compensated for it later on 27 November.

Opposite: January 1940, and already petrol rationing is having an effect. One small car is parked in Vine Street outside the Randall's building which opened in May 1939.

Britain's first propaganda film, *The Lion Has Wings*, was made in a record time of twelve days at nearby Denham Studios and shown at the Odeon from Monday 27 November for a week. On the first night, one of its stars, June Duprez, made a personal appearance to promote the film, but not knowing the time of her entrance, I sat in the stalls for five hours and watched the whole programme twice, while waiting to see her. Suddenly a torch flashed in my face, and there was an usherette with my father, calling me out. Walking up the aisle, I mumbled an explanation, whereupon the sympathetic girl asked him if he would like to wait and see Miss Duprez – about to appear on stage. He agreed; we were shown into the back row; and I got away with a telling off.

Meanwhile in New Mill, my mother had become increasingly homesick and decided to return home before Christmas 1939 with the rest of the family. Almost three quarters of evacuees throughout the country were reunited with their parents at the same time. Nevertheless, this first wartime Christmas was not exactly a merry one. Petrol rationing had been introduced in October and food ration books were distributed in December as a reminder of what was to come when rationing started in the New Year. Then snow came and continued for two months. With it came freezing temperatures.

So the decade came to an end on a rather depressing and pessimistic note. The 1930s had witnessed turbulent times both in Britain and around the world. No one could foresee exactly what the future held in store, but it was certainly looking like an even worse scenario.

As another harsh winter ushered in 1940, I started at my new school in Gunnersbury as the staff and pupils had returned from their brief evacuation to Chesham. While they were away, a large area under the assembly-hall stage had been reinforced as had some of the classrooms, and a semi-underground shelter was sited in the playground. School hours were much curtailed and

for the first year we attended on only four half-days a week, with Wednesday afternoons reserved for sport. Two of my classmates went on to make names for themselves after the war – Kenneth Haigh from Hayes became a noted TV, film and stage actor, while the late Patrick Chesterman from Ealing was Senior Orthopaedic Surgeon of the Royal Berkshire Hospital, Reading. His department was among the most advanced in Britain.

Back at St Mary's, similar reinforcements had been made to the main corridor, cloakrooms and staff room – chosen to act as shelters. By February 1940, school hours had reverted to normal, only to be severely disrupted by the Blitz in September, when pupils were allowed to start at 10.30 a.m. after all-night raids. During daytime raids, children were entertained by schoolfellows Josie and Wally Twomey playing piano accordions. While at Wood End Park Junior School in Hayes, a girl named Joan Dowling sang to pupils in the underground shelter during air-raid drills. Later, as a teenager, she became well known in British films after playing a leading role in *No Room At The Inn*. In September 1940, St Mary's received another two buckets, a stirrup pump and a lantern to add to their solitary bucket and shovel. When twenty-five sandbags arrived shortly afterwards, they must have wondered what they had done to deserve it!

From the beginning of 1940, it became evident that the name of the game was austerity, and on 8 January food rationing was imposed for the first time since 1918. We were required to register with a specific grocer and butcher of our own choosing, and each person's weekly allowance was 4oz of butter, 4oz of bacon or ham, 12oz of sugar and two eggs.

Meat was rationed from 11 March, the individual allocation being 1s 10d worth per week and in July, tea, margarine and other fats joined the list. Vegetables were plentiful as the public responded to the government's persistent urging to 'dig for victory' and 'grow your own food'.

Above: The Masonic Hall, New Windsor Street, where a 'pillbox' machine-gun post disguised as a chapel was erected near the front of the building.

A view from the bridge of the River Frays flowing downstream from Fountain's Mill. On the extreme right is family friend Reg Twinn's greengrocery shop, which, in 1910, was the town's first cinema, Rockingham Hall.

The machine-gun section of Uxbridge Home Guard in June 1941. Obviously the days of sharing one rifle between a whole platoon had long gone!

Opposite below: Rockingham Bridge, built in 1809 and widened in 1895 at a cost of £365. An original 5ton weight-limit sign was removed in 1939 to allow heavy military vehicles to cross, and the bridge was prepared to accommodate tank traps to counter the invasion threat.

The Ministry of Food issued countless recipes, backed by advertisements in newspapers headed 'Food Facts', and on cinema screens titled 'Food Flashes'. These usually featured vegetables as the main ingredients and we were continually being given tips like '101 things to do with carrots'. A slight exaggeration perhaps, but you get the idea. Tins of dried egg powder were a reasonable substitute for the real thing and made quite acceptable omelettes, while a year later a new word entered the vocabulary when tins of Spam arrived from America.

Around the town further changes were taking place. The iron railings in front of our gardens and other buildings, parks and recreation grounds were removed for munitions, a 'pillbox' (machine-gun post) disguised as a small chapel was erected at the end of our road in New Windsor Street, and on Rockingham Bridge a few yards away, holes were dug to accommodate tank traps, in the event of an invasion.

An important event affecting the whole nation was the formation of the Local Defence Volunteers (LDV) instigated by Anthony Eden on 14 May 1940. Mr Eden had been recalled by the Prime Minister as soon as the war began, and Winston Churchill became First Lord of the Admiralty again in a Cabinet reshuffle. 250,000 men between the ages of seventeen and sixty-five volunteered to join the new anti-invasion force during the first week, and in Uxbridge, enrolment at the Drill Hall was encouraging. A large property called The Shrubbery in the High Street, was taken over as 'B' Company, 14th Batallion Middlesex Home Guard Headquarters, while some of our local factories had formed units of their own.

Prominent among them was the Bell Punch Co., who were actively engaged on war work producing many electro-mechanical devices for the Admiralty and Air Ministry. The Uxbridge

'A' Company, 14th Middlesex Battalion Home Guard at their Church Farm, Ickenham headquarters. Like their Uxbridge counterparts, they are displaying a cup awarded for shooting skills.

Above: Local Home Guard units formed part of a 'Wings For Victory' parade through Uxbridge on 6 March 1943. The procession is seen here in Wellington Road.

Right: Certificate awarded to Uxbridge Home Guard Sgt Frank Clay after the force was disbanded in December 1944. Frank had lost an arm while serving in the Army during the First World War.

In the years when our Country was in mortal danger

FRANK CLAY

who served 16 January 1941 - 31 December 1944

gave generously of his time and powers to make himself ready for her defence by force of arms and with his life if need be.

THE HOME GUARD

Army drivers and their Bren Gun carriers with staff of Norman Reeves Motors, George Street. The firm's workforce spent the war years overhauling and servicing these vehicles.

Our local shops on this parade in Cowley Road seem well protected against bomb blast in October 1940.

Rear view of our house in How's Road. The downstairs window, bottom right, was covered with corrugated-iron shutters every night during the Blitz.

Electric Supply Co. (Metesco) also had its own Home Guard unit – the new name of the LDV, suggested by Churchill who became Prime Minister following Neville Chamberlain's resignation on 10 May.

Aside from rationing and shortages of practically every commodity, we were subjected to all kinds of restrictions. We were urged to use only 5in of hot water when bathing, although I doubt if any inspectors with rulers were on hand to measure the depth! One regulation that was religiously enforced concerned the blackout, in place since 1 September 1939. One of the most familiar sounds at the time was a loud yell of 'Put that light out!' from the air-raid wardens – often accompanied by some colourful adjectives! Car headlights, cycle lamps and torches all had to be masked to deflect their light downwards and householders were responsible for blacking out all windows with thick, black, canvas-type material. The drapers' shops did a roaring trade! Some people, including shopkeepers, barricaded the outside of their windows with shutters. My father had a set of corrugated-iron sheets made by a workmate to fit our living-room window. Despite having two handles on each sheet, they were extremely heavy to lift, and it took two of us to hoist them on to hooks in the wall, before securing them with wing nuts.

At this point, the government's two main fears were attacks from the air, maybe with mustard gas, and the constant threat of invasion. To counteract the latter, all signposts throughout the country were removed, railway station name-boards were painted over (except on the London Underground), place names on lorries and other transport received similar treatment, and all kinds of makeshift obstacles were positioned on roads and in fields to make things difficult for the invader. This exercise and other duties ensured that the veterans and youngsters of the newly formed 'Dads Army' (a much later nickname for the Home Guard) were kept busy. But the missing place names also made it difficult for everyone – even the military had trouble

Uxbridge Sanitary Laundry in Laundry Yard. The town's name has been obliterated in keeping with wartime regulations.

Cars are still conspicuous by their absence in the High Street. In fact the policeman on point duty is holding up non-existent traffic to allow pedestrians across the road!

A similar situation in Station Road, West Drayton. The only signs of life are two cyclists, a motorbike and sidecar, and two small vehicles. An air-raid siren is mounted on the tall post by Lloyds Bank next to the Police Box.

driving around unfamiliar territory. And the blackout had already caused an alarming number of road accidents and fatalities, while, on 30 December, a man fell from an 80-ft viaduct between Uxbridge and Denham after stepping out of a train that he thought had stopped at a station.

But it wasn't all doom and gloom. Our spirits were constantly lifted and our morale boosted by the escapist entertainment available. Apart from the cinema, the radio (which we always referred to as the wireless) now came into its own as it provided a variety of comedy shows and music, in addition to the eagerly awaited news bulletins. Because of the blackout and danger of air-raids, more people were forced to stay indoors at night, and were well catered for by the BBC. Whole families huddled round their sets every evening lapping up comedy programmes like *Band Waggon, Monday Night at Eight, Garrison Theatre* and the most popular of all, *It's That Man Again* or ITMA as it was commonly known. The latter's catchphrases became part of the language. We were in the middle of the Big Band era, and seemed to have as many in Britain as America, and consequently we were treated to several broadcasts a day, although there was plenty of classical music for those who preferred it. Our wireless was operated by a heavy 'Exide' type battery and an acid accumulator which needed recharging periodically. It was my job to take it to Tommy Rose's cycle shop in New Windsor Street where it was put on charge for forty-eight hours at a cost of 6d. We did not always have a spare, and that meant no wireless for two days.

The songwriters had also been playing their part in keeping the nation cheerful and stirring its emotions from day one of the war. Earlier, in fact, when in the summer of 1939, the Lancashire lassie Gracie Fields, known affectionately as 'Our Gracie', starred in the film *Shipyard Sally* which featured the hit song 'Wish Me Luck (As You Wave Me Goodbye)'. When war began, it immediately took on a new significance as thousands of servicemen were leaving their families for overseas destinations. Soon afterwards, Vera Lynn, who would become known as the 'Forces Sweetheart', introduced another big favourite 'We'll Meet Again'. It superseded 'Wish Me Luck', as the goodbyes had been said, and the new sentiments focused on looking forward to future reunions. Later, another great wartime favourite emerged – 'There'll Always Be An England', which seemed to epitomise all that the country stood for and capture the mood of the nation. Its patriotic lyrics and stirring tune virtually replaced 'Land Of Hope And Glory' as our second national anthem and was sung with an almost religious fervour that made the hair stand up on the back of the neck. 200,000 copies of the sheet music were sold within two months of its publication.

In addition to these patriotic and sentimental melodies, there were plenty of songs with a comic flavour, among them 'We're Gonna Hang Out The Washing On The Siegfried Line', 'Kiss Me Goodnight Sergeant Major ' and 'In The Quartermaster's Stores'. Other songs popular with the Army were 'Bless 'em All', 'Roll Out The Barrel', 'Run Rabbit, Run' and a lively tune written for the Army Film Unit's propaganda documentary *Troopship* titled 'Hold Your Hats On'. The music was composed by Richard Addinsell, whose 'Warsaw Concerto' from the film *Dangerous Moonlight* became an instant classical favourite.

Among the comic songs were several featuring Hitler, the most popular being 'Adolf' by John Mills' sister, Annette, and 'Der Fuhrer's Face'. He was constantly depicted as a figure of fun in newspaper cartoons and children's comics. Youngsters made up their own songs about him such as this, which was sung to the Walt Disney tune from *Snow White and the Seven Dwarfs*:

> Whistle while you work
> Hitler is a twerp
> Goering's barmy, so's his army
> Rub 'em in the dirt!

It echoed our songs in 1936 during the Italian-Abyssinian war when we poked fun at the dictator Benito Mussolini. Our parody had somewhat ruder words and was sung to the tune of 'Roll Along Covered Wagon':

> Roll along Mussolini, roll along
> You won't be in Abyssinia very long
> You'll be lying on the grass
> With a bullet up your ****
> Roll along Mussolini, roll along!

Another form of ridicule appeared in the form of a children's game consisting of a dart board bearing a large picture of Hitler's rear instead of numbers. It came complete with a set of darts for you to throw at the target, while his face even appeared on toilet rolls. What would they think of next?

Up to May 1940, none of the anticipated enemy action had materialised and consequently the period from 3 September 1939 was labelled as the 'phoney war'. In fact, it was literally the lull before the storm, and when the storm broke, all hell was let loose on the Home Front. There was nothing phoney about what followed.

The reality of war was brought home to everyone on 27 May when all eyes focused on the beaches of Dunkirk where the British Expeditionary Forces (BEF) were fighting a desperate rearguard action. After Holland and then Belgium had capitulated to the Nazis, the Germans encircled the BEF in a pincer-type movement, forcing them to retreat towards the sea. It was then that the Royal Navy launched Operation Dynamo, attempting the greatest maritime rescue of all time. Every type of seagoing vessel imaginable was employed in the exercise, many of them piloted by civilians. Protection from the air was provided by the RAF, who lost 100 planes in the process, but the end result was that over 368,000 soldiers were brought safely home, where they would live to fight another day. The miracle of Dunkirk had been accomplished.

On 31 May, the leader of the British Fascist Party, Oswald Mosley who lived just outside Uxbridge at Savay Farm, Denham was arrested and interned. Mosley had been a frequent Saturday night soap box orator at our so called 'Speaker's Corner' behind the Market House during the 1930s. He was released, amid much protest, in November 1943.

We were now entering what was probably one of the most dramatic and decisive periods of the war, at least on the Home Front. After the German Luftwaffe had attacked RAF airfields in South East England with considerable success for some months, it now turned its attention to London.

The Battle of Britain was about to begin.

'Never in the field of human conflict was so much owed by so many to so few' said Prime Minister Churchill to General Hastings Ismay as they left the Operations Room at RAF Uxbridge on 16 August 1940. It had been a particularly successful day for the Fighter Command pilots who had shot down a record number (seventy-five) of German aircraft. On 20 August, the Premier repeated his remarks in a speech to the House of Commons, after which he received a standing ovation.

The entrance to the underground Operations Room at RAF Uxbridge.

Left: Interior of the 'bunker' showing some of the seventy-six steps.

Opposite above: 'Park House' at RAF Uxbridge, home of AVM Park, Air Officer Commanding No. 11 Group.

Opposite below: The controllers' position, showing the curved glass screen installed in 1939.

Work on the underground Operations Room began in late 1938, and it became operational just ten days before the outbreak of war. In fact it was one of several rooms 60ft below ground and reached by seventy-six steps. Descending into the depths is quite an eerie experience – the air is dank and musty, and thoughts of famous figures from the past inevitably come to mind. Churchill, of course, was a frequent visitor, and others included King George VI and Queen Elizabeth II, Lord Mountbatten, Field Marshal Montgomery and Generals Eisenhower and de Gaulle.

RAF Uxbridge was the headquarters of No. 11 Group, the first regional group to be set up by ACM Sir Hugh Dowding from his Fighter Command headquarters at Stanmore, a few miles away. It was to act as the hub and nerve centre through which up to the minute information would be channelled relating to the strength, position and course of approaching enemy aircraft. It thus played a vital role in the defence of Britain from air attack. The group commander was AVM Keith Park, a New Zealander who had previously been Station Commander at nearby RAF Northolt. A large number of personnel was required to man the control room (often referred to as the 'bunker') many of whom were WAAFs (Woman's Royal Auxilliary Air Force) who worked at the plotting table. One of these was Betty (née Giles) Kingston who had enlisted in 1940. She was posted to Uxbridge and subsequently promoted to sergeant in charge of one of the watches. Betty spent the rest of the war doing this job, during which time she met the King

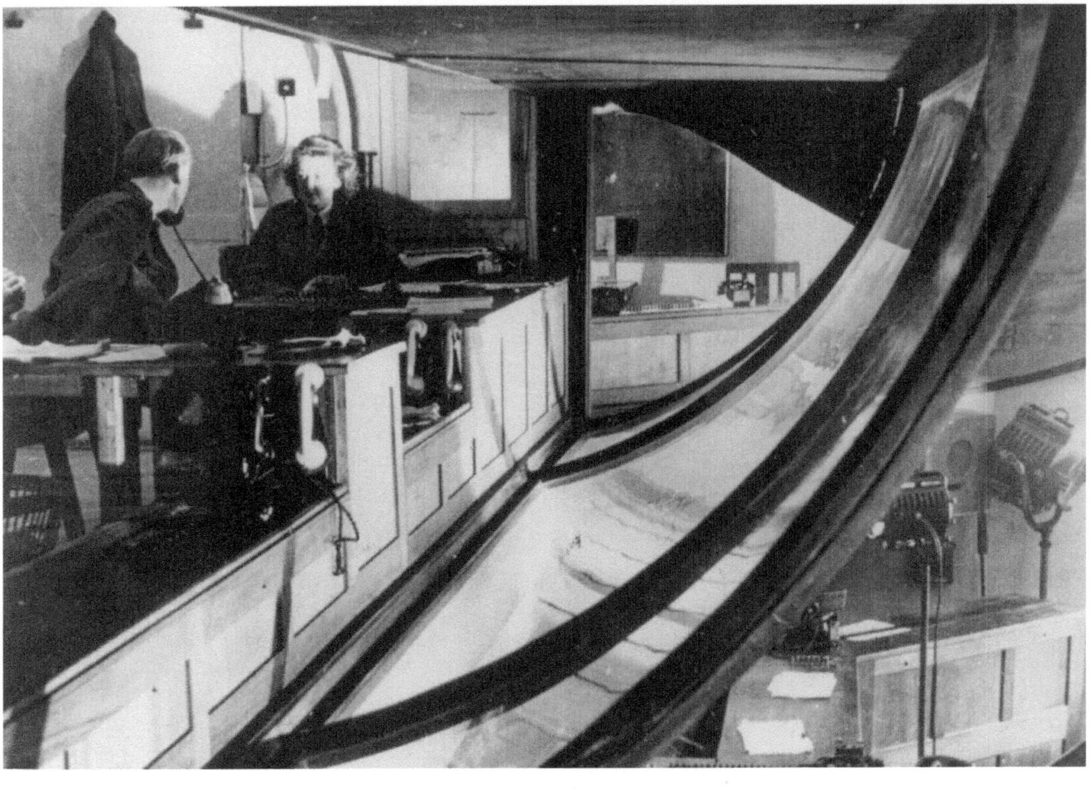

RAF and WAAF Operations personnel in the plotting room.

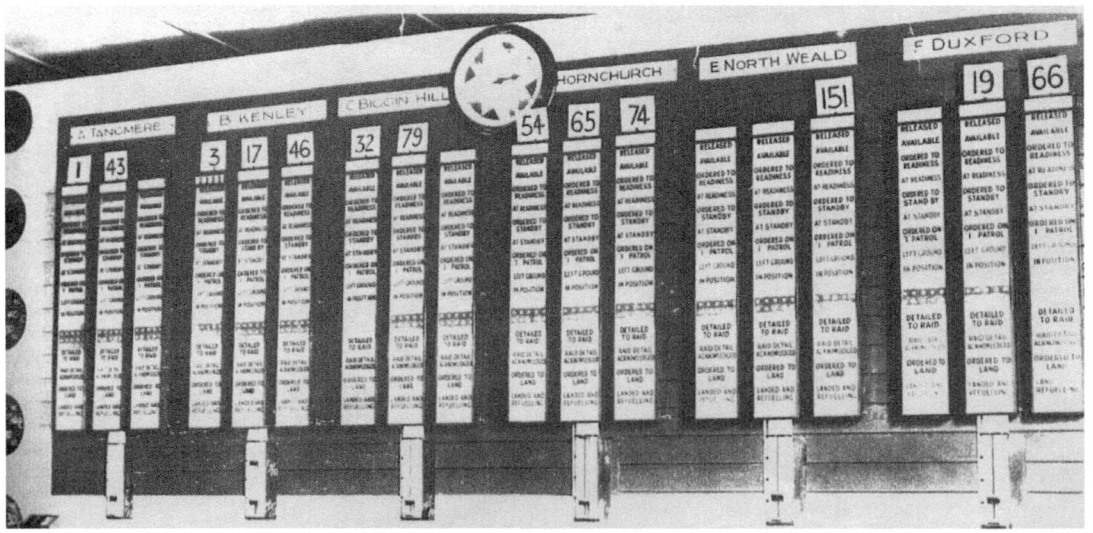

The illuminated 'Tote Board' covering an entire wall of the plotting room, which showed the readiness states and deployment of Hurricane and Spitfire squadrons of 11 Group.

Above: Former enemies get together at the Operations Room in 1979. Lord (former Wg Cdr) Willoughby de Broke, the Senior Controller on the memorable Sunday 15 September 1940 shows the plotting table to ex-Luftwaffe pilots. On his left is Feldwebel Wilhelm Raab who took part in the morning raid on that day. This was one of several visits to the 'bunker' by German aircrew.

Right: Sergeant Betty (née Giles) Kingston who worked in the Operations Room from 1940-1945.

and Queen, and in 1945 she married and decided to stay in the area, settling at New Denham. She was made a life member of the Uxbridge History Society after serving on its committee for twenty-five years, and died in 2002.

Also working on the station in a hut near the 'bunker' was Uxbridge girl Pamela (née Foster) Holden. She was a shorthand typist in the Organisation Branch of HQ 11 Group from 1940-1944. AVM Park often worked in the building, and Pamela described him as 'a most charming man who always acknowledged the humble clerks and typists'. Other staff included comedian Douglas 'Cardew' Robinson and film director Lewis Gilbert. Celebrities always seemed to be around, and in 1943 Sqn Ldr Rex Harrison and film actors Cyril Raymond and Ronald Adam all worked in the Operations Room. Pamela also met secret agent Yvonne Baseden, who featured in two television documentaries. She remembers the visits of Mr Churchill and the King and Queen, when the staff was told to stay away from the windows facing the 'bunker', which she always called the 'hole'. However, on 16 August, her colleague Alice Munden another Uxbridge girl, ignored instructions and went outside to watch the Prime Minister alight from his car. Pamela was posted to Gloucester in April 1944, and could not have envisaged the tragic incident that would necessitate her return to Uxbridge two months later.

On Sunday 15 September 1940, Mr Churchill and his wife who had spent the weekend at Chequers, decided to call in at 11 Group HQ on their way back to London. As they went below to the Operations Room, AVM Park remarked to the PM that as everything was quiet at present, he didn't know if anything would happen that day. Perhaps it was just as well, since that day

Betty on a return visit to the 'bunker' in 1987 with WO Chris Wren (since retired) at the Operations Room memorial.

The 'guardian' of the main gate at RAF Uxbridge. This aircraft is a replica of a MK 9 Spitfire as flown by 64 Squadron from Hornchurch, Essex in 1942.

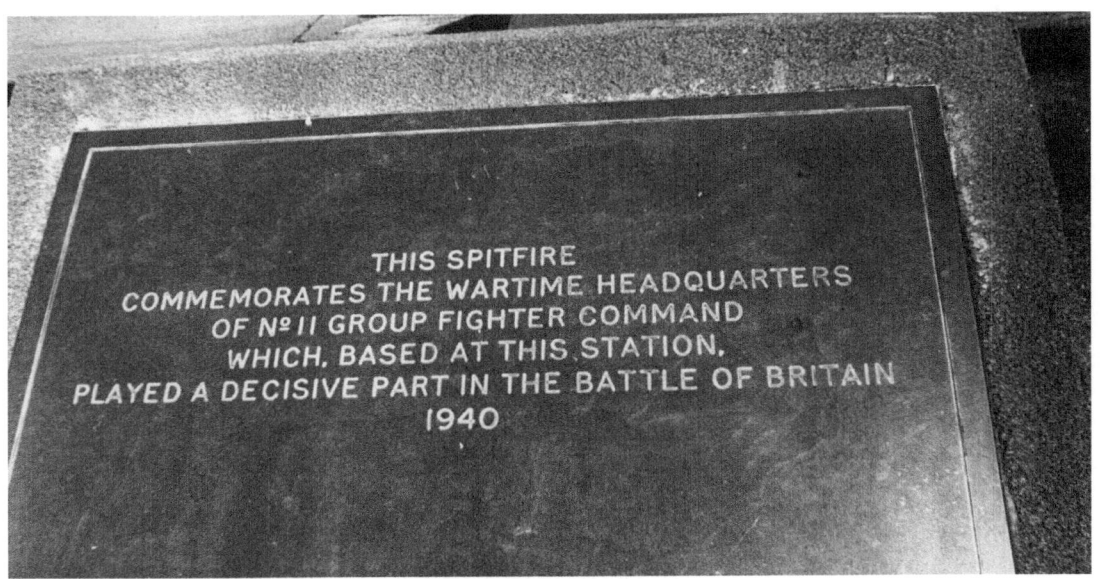

THIS SPITFIRE
COMMEMORATES THE WARTIME HEADQUARTERS
OF No 11 GROUP FIGHTER COMMAND
WHICH, BASED AT THIS STATION,
PLAYED A DECISIVE PART IN THE BATTLE OF BRITAIN
1940

The memorial stone under the aeroplane's propeller.

John and Bobby Baker shortly before their sea voyage which ended in disaster.

Reich Marshal Goering decided to launch the Luftwaffe's biggest ever daylight raid. This came in the form of two separate attacks in the morning and afternoon. Almost 350 German bombers and fighters were deployed in the first of these, and even more in the second. As usual the RAF pilots were outnumbered by two or three to one, but also as usual, Fighter Command came out on top. In the afternoon raid the squadrons in 11 Group were reinforced by those from East Anglia's 12 Group led by Sqn Ldr Douglas Bader and, by the end of the day, the Luftwaffe had suffered a most humiliating defeat. Initially the number of German losses was announced on the radio and in the next day's newspapers as 185. In fact it was sixty with many more damaged, while the RAF had lost twenty-six aircraft.

The day's proceedings had been followed intently by Mr and Mrs Churchill who sat in what Mr Churchill called the 'dress circle' looking down on the plotting table. Later, in his war memoirs, he likened the control room to a small theatre. Standing next to the Churchills was the Senior Controller, Wg Cdr Lord Willoughby de Broke who directed the whole operation, while Keith Park paced up and down behind them, occasionally intervening with an order and also communicating with Sir Hugh Dowding at Command HQ, Stanmore.

As a result of the day's events, Hitler was forced to acknowledge that he could not gain supremacy of the skies over Britain – the essential precursor to his planned invasion – and on 17 September he postponed 'Operation Sealion' (the invasion's code name), cancelling it completely a month later. Although the 'Battle of Britain' was ongoing until 31 October 1940, the turning point was undoubtedly 15 September which was destined to become known as Battle of Britain Day.

Not only was it the turning point of the battle, but in all probability one of the turning points of the whole war.

Two days before that decisive Sunday, the Indian liner SS *City of Benares* carrying 406 passengers and crew, sailed out of Liverpool heading for Canada. It was Friday 13 September

Above: Entrance to RAF Northolt, the nearest airfield to Uxbridge.
No. 303 Squadron, based here, was comprised of Polish pilots who had fled from the Nazis. They accounted for 126 enemy aircraft, and the Polish War Memorial on the A40 is a lasting tribute to them. Off duty, they frequented the Orchard Hotel, Ruislip and dances at St Catherine's Hall, West Drayton, where the band honoured them by playing their national anthem after our own.

Right: Joy Wooster with her father, a Hillingdon air-raid warden, a year after the tragedy.

1940. On board were ninety evacuee children including Bobby and John Baker from Southall. Their mother Lucy and Alice Wooster of Colham Green, Hillingdon had been firm friends since their working days at the HMV Gramophone Co. in Hayes. Lucy had arranged with the Children's Overseas Reception Board (CORB) for her two sons to be evacuated to Canada, and suggested that Alice send her daughter Joy with them. But after spending several sleepless nights contemplating the issue, Alice sought a neighbour's advice and as a result, decided not to be separated from her only child.

At 10.00 p.m. on 17 September, the ship was 600 miles out in the tempestuous mid-Atlantic when it suffered a direct hit from a single torpedo. It was fired by the German Unterseeboot 48, which, in its first two years of service, had established a record number of fifty-five 'kills'. In pitch darkness and buffeted by a ferocious gale, the storm-tossed City of Benares began to list almost immediately and sank within twenty minutes. Seven year old John Baker saw his older brother Bobby try to climb into a lifeboat, only to miss his footing and fall to his death under the sinking ship. Minutes earlier, Bobby had passed his lifejacket to John who was one of only seven children rescued by warship HMS *Hurricane*, although eight days later a lifeboat carrying another six evacuees was picked up by HMS *Anthony*. But in the meantime, 211 adults and seventy-seven children, including four from Hillingdon, had perished in the ice-cold sea. Those from Hillingdon were Enid Butlin, Audrey Muncey, Beryl Myatt and Colense Rodda.

Shortly after receiving the traumatic news of her son's death, Lucy's hair turned white. How she must have wished that she had made the same decision as her friend. As for Joy who missed the boat that sank on her twelfth birthday, it was obviously a very lucky break for her. Lucky for me also, as our paths crossed five years later, and we married in 1949.

Three years on from the *City of Benares* sinking. Survivor John with his mother (far left) and father. The other ladies are Joy's grandmother and mother.

At the time when the Battle of Britain was reaching its height, the Blitz began in earnest on 7 September 1940, although London had suffered its first bombing a fortnight earlier on 24 August. The Germans embarked on a strategy of concentrated night raids, and consequently the civilians' nightly routine followed a regular pattern. Those with back-garden Anderson shelters prepared to go underground armed with hot water-bottles, thermos flasks, torches, candles, matches, reading material and playing cards. With my family it was getting ready to bed down for the night in the cupboard under the stairs, known for as long as I can remember as 'the dog's cupboard'. Apart from housing the gas meter, it had been home to my grandmother's dog Judy until she had to be put down after taking a fancy to the meter-reader's leg and biting a chunk out of it. Anyway, the name stuck. In fact, my grandmother never slept anywhere but in her own bed. She did come downstairs on a couple of occasions when a particularly heavy bombardment was in progress. But it wasn't to sleep as she was dressed in her overcoat and hat, and carried a small attaché case which I imagine contained her most precious possessions. She then sat in a chair until things quietened down and went back to bed. My father was part of the street fire-watching team and was out on patrol during most of the night raids.

At roughly the same time each evening came the mournful wail of the sirens, filling us with a sinking feeling, while searchlights probed the sky in continuous sweeping movements. How long would it be until the bombers arrived? Not very long usually, before we heard the distinctive intermittent drone of German engines. Our hearts pounded as they flew overhead, and we prayed that they would keep going without unloading their lethal cargo. Thankfully, more often than not they did, although that meant that some other locality would suffer instead. Other waves would usually follow at intervals, and often we heard them again on their return flight. All the while a continuous barrage of shellfire made much more noise than the aircraft. The nearest 'ack-ack' (anti-aircraft) battery, nicknamed 'Big Bertha', was sited at Chandler's Hill on the Uxbridge-Iver border, while across the road in the recreation ground was a smaller Bofors gun emplacement. We soon learned to distinguish between the sound of shells and exploding bombs.

On the night of 28 September, a bomb fell on houses in Rockingham Parade, just two streets away from us. Six people including a ten-year-old boy were killed, and rescue teams spent hours saving others from the wreckage. Later, wardens Norman Petts and Jack Livesey were awarded the 'George Medal' for working all night to rescue an elderly man from the debris. Some days earlier, a seventeen-year-old youth and an eight-month-old baby died in two separate bombings in Hillingdon.

Then, on 6 October, as we were about to eat Sunday lunch, I was washing my hands at the kitchen sink when I heard a sudden 'whoosh' – a weird rushing sound directly overhead, followed by the thud of an explosion not very far away. It was one of a stick of bombs and the most damaging, as it destroyed a row of cottages in Montague Road and partly demolished a nearby chapel. The death toll was eight adults, a seven-year-old girl and an eight-month-old baby. A week later, on 14 October, more bombs fell across Uxbridge, one of them destroying two bungalows at Willowbank, Denham. Ironically, a twelve-year-old boy, one of 100 evacuees from Stepney, London, was killed in what had been deemed a 'safe' area. Another bomb fell in the grounds of Sanderson's Fabrics Co., the blast blowing out windows of Frays College in Harefield Road, and resulting in pupils spending several days wearing overcoats in the classrooms.

Around 9.15 p.m. on Thursday 7 November, yet another cluster of bombs was unleashed on the town, causing four fatalities, the first being a man who died from injuries after one dropped in Rockingham Recreation Ground, not far from our house. Two more landed almost side by side – one on Randall's car park and the other on the Savoy Cinema opposite, where it hit the front facade and lodged in the roof. As usual when the sirens sounded, a message to this effect

Aftermath of the bomb on Rockingham Parade which killed Betty Eves, Elizabeth Garland, Walter Taylor, William and Louisa Laws and their ten-year-old son Billy.

Remains of two bungalows on the Willowbank Estate, New Denham in which a twelve-year-old evacuee Peter Field was killed.

Above and below: Volunteers clearing debris after the Montague Road bombing. The ten fatalities were Mr and Mrs S. Brown, their daughter Iris, Mr and Mrs A. Gadbury, Mr and Mrs H. Thatcher, Mrs Metcalfe, her daughter Anne and Miss D. Godfrey.

Staff inspecting bomb damage at the rear of Randall's building.

CENSORED!

We take this opportunity of announcing that as a ▬▬ ▬▬ ▬▬ ▬▬ ▬▬ ▬▬ ▬▬ ▬▬ ▬▬ but we are able to assure the public we still maintain the Excellent Service which is expected of

RANDALLS
of UXBRIDGE
COMPLETE HOUSE FURNISHERS
TELEPHONE UX. 1500

FURNITURE : SOFT FURNISHINGS : CARPETS : LINOS CUTLERY : GLASS & HARDWARE : AIR RAID SHELTER REQUISITES ETC

(Original advert from the Gazette of November 1940 assuring customers of normal service despite the store suffering bomb damage.)

The store's newspaper advertisement, heavily censored, following the bombing.

The Savoy Cinema had a lucky escape when a bomb lodged in the roof, causing minimal damage.

had been projected on to the screen, and also as usual, the audience all stayed put. A full house had just enjoyed a Laurel and Hardy comedy *Saps at Sea*, and were watching *Edison the Man* when the bomb struck. According to an *Advertiser and Gazette* report, they were so absorbed in the film, that they took little notice of the explosion. Up in the projection box, a fourteen-year-old trainee Anthony Stagg was hit on the head by a piece of metal, but carried on manfully assisting his chief Mr J. Maloney. Between them they ensured that the film continued running without interruption until the end. Although no one in the cinema was injured, an elderly lady and her son living opposite died from the bomb blast, and an RAF serviceman walking in the High Street was killed by flying glass. Other bombs from the same stick fell near Montague Road and on the Casualty Station alongside the swimming pool.

Some time earlier, a few miles away at West Ealing, my Aunt Mary had a lucky escape when her house and others in Talbot Road were demolished. As her husband was on night work and her daughter, a nurse, was on duty at a local hospital, she had stayed overnight with her sister at Hanwell. When she returned the next morning, she found the road cordoned off and a pile of rubble where her home had been.

Furthermore, on the evening of 29 November, one of my Gunnersbury classmates, Anthony Roche, who lived opposite the school, had just reached the playground shelter used by local residents, when his house received a direct hit, killing both his parents.

The late autumn had seen hundreds of bombs (mainly incendiary devices) showered on Hillingdon, West Drayton and neighbouring areas. The night of Saturday 16 November was West Drayton's turn for a concentrated attack consisting mainly of fire bombs and a few explosives. St Catherine's rectory and parish hall were hit, along with a factory, shops and houses, but fortunately there were no casualties. One incendiary had pierced the roof of the hall and failed to ignite. It was discovered on the next morning by a young parishioner, Bobby Harris, who was

Above: A scene of devastation at the ambulance station adjacent to Uxbridge Swimming Pool.

Left: RAF pilot Bobby Harris who was killed at the age of twenty-one.

helping to prepare for the regular Sunday-night dance. Obviously not well trained in ARP, he picked it up and cycled towards home with one hand on his handlebars and the other clutching the bomb. On the way he met the hall social secretary Ned Smyth with his daughter Phil Jarvis, and asked a horrified Ned 'What shall I do with this?' Phil remembered that her father had told him in no uncertain terms to find the nearest sand bucket. A year later, Bobby trained as a pilot in the RAF, and sadly, was shot down and killed in 1943 at the age of twenty-one. The 16 November had been a harrowing experience for West Drayton residents, but the people of Hamburg fared much worse, as that night the RAF dropped 2,000 bombs on the city in its biggest raid since the outbreak of war.

With the advent of the New Year 1941, the raids became less frequent, and thus it was ironic that we were then allocated an indoor Morrison shelter, named after Home Secretary Herbert Morrison. It was a heavy, steel construction with wire-mesh sides and took up most of the living room, but was rarely used for its intended purpose. From day one, it had doubled as a dining table and also proved ideal for playing table tennis. Similarly, the outdoor brick shelter in How's Close also had another use as it acted as a goal for football and bicycle polo games. All it needed were two white-chalk marks for the goal posts.

By May 1941, the civilian population was able to enjoy a welcome respite from the continual aerial bombardment by the Luftwaffe, but not before the Germans left London a final calling card on the night of 10 May, killing 1,436 people and injuring another 1,752. The city which had borne the brunt of the offensive since the Blitz began was bombed on fifty-seven consecutive nights in addition to many daytime raids. Britain's other major cities were also regular targets – in particular Coventry, where 554 people died on the night of 14 November 1940.

When reflecting on the Blitz period, what emerges as truly amazing is the resilience and fortitude shown by the ordinary man and woman in the street. The people were united in a way they had never been before and probably never will be again. They not only showed great courage in the face of adversity, but also displayed a wonderful sense of humour which preserved some kind of sanity in a crazy world. An appropriate new phrase 'The Blitz Spirit' came into the language, a much used slogan 'Britain Can Take It' was no exaggeration, and as Winston Churchill said later, 'This was their finest hour'.

So life went on, and gradually, a touch of normality returned – apart, of course, from the austerity of the times. A further reminder was the introduction of clothes rationing on 1 June 1941. My school hours reverted to normal and we now attended on Saturday mornings to compensate for the time lost in 1940. More time was made up by having only one extra day holiday at Whitsun each year, and the summer holiday being restricted to an exact four weeks. Lessons were still interrupted by sporadic daytime raids and on 30 January 1941 we were confined in an indoor classroom shelter for almost five hours. On another occasion a raid had started while I was on the train journey to school. On reaching my station I saw the display-board notice indicating that the air-raid alert had been sounded, but as I was already late due to the train being delayed, I decided to start the twenty-minute walk to school rather than take cover. There was an eerie silence and the roads were completely deserted. I had almost reached the school when I heard the tell-tale drone of a German engine, and looking up, saw a lone aircraft overhead. Within seconds it had passed over, and I ran the rest of the way with my heart thumping wildly.

June 1941 saw the introduction of 'Double Summer Time', giving us an extra hour of daylight, with sunset at around 10.20 p.m. It meant that we could play cricket until 10 p.m. and then call at Mr Adams' general shop in The Lynch which remained 'open all hours', to buy cold drinks after the game.

As time went by, a more relaxed atmosphere prevailed, and people grasped every opportunity to try and forget the war. There was plenty of entertainment on offer – dancing at three venues in the High Street, Burton's hall above their men's tailoring shop, the Regal Cinema and Express Dairy ballrooms, and several church halls. Picture-going was still the most popular pastime for all ages and cinema queues were longer than those outside the food shops. I became an avid film fan and clocked up 147 visits during 1941 followed by 176 in 1942. Some might call that a misspent youth! Even at the cinema, however, we could not escape from the war completely, as the newsreels, which ran two editions every week, kept us abreast of events abroad and consisted almost entirely of war news.

In May 1941, my friend Don Mead, then aged fourteen, started work at the nearby Ambassador Cinema in Hayes, and began his projectionist training by showing the newsreel. He told me that the management invited families who had seen any relative in a newsreel to a private showing on the following morning. He recalled a poignant occasion when a group arrived to have another viewing of their father who had appeared in a news item on the previous day. Poignant because, before leaving the house, they had received a telegram saying he had been killed in action.

Further entertainment was provided by our Odeon cinema, which staged a number of Sunday-afternoon charity concerts. Oscar Deutsch, king of the Odeon empire had generously allowed the theatre to be used at no cost, and guest stars willingly gave their services free of charge. I attended the first concert on 20 October 1940 in aid of the local Spitfire fund, and the artistes included Greta Gynt, Valerie Hobson, David Tree and Leonard Henry, who compèred the show. Other concerts followed, some featuring the RAF Dance Orchestra (the Squadronaires), stationed at Uxbridge throughout the war. Led by Sgt Jimmy Miller, the band comprised many well known musicians who, in peacetime, had played in the top orchestras of the day. They

'The Squadronaires', RAF Dance Orchestra in concert. The line up includes Sid Colin, Jimmy Miller (leader), Andy McDevitt, George Chisholm and Jimmy Durante.

Another concert featuring Sid Colin (guitar), Jock Cummings (drums), and Ronnie Aldrich (piano), whose children were pupils at St Mary's.

included Tommy McQuater, George Chisholm, Kenny Baker, Sid Phillips, Jimmy Durante, Andy McDevitt, Sid Colin, Jock Cummings and Ronnie Aldrich. When they were not working, many of the band members could be seen having morning coffee in Pam's Pantry, a High Street tea shop which they seemed to frequent quite regularly. Most of their time, however, was occupied with a busy working schedule which included radio broadcasts and touring military bases and variety theatres.

Other well-known faces were sometimes spotted in the town, including actors and actresses who had homes in the surrounding area and often worked at Denham Studios. In late 1939, Valerie Hobson, who lived at Gerrards Cross, bought a bicycle at Curry's shop in the High Street as part of a publicity drive to save petrol. Miss Hobson was also a regular visitor to the Odeon, as were John Mills and Jimmy Hanley, who both lived at Denham. Finlay Currie from Gerrards Cross was another patron of the Odeon, and because he said he couldn't see from the back seats, always sat in the front stalls and gave the usherette a 1s tip. I saw him regularly on Sunday mornings as he attended the Roman Catholic church, as did actress Mary Morris who lived in a flat opposite. She had just finished making *The Thief of Baghdad*, and then starred in 'Pimpernel Smith'. Another character actor who often worshipped there was Noel Purcell.

Occasionally, I had a glimpse of other film actors when helping out my mother's greengrocer on her rounds during the school holidays and Saturdays. She owned a smallholding on the Oxford Road at Denham and supplied the studio canteens. In those days film making went on seven days a week, so we were quite likely to spot a famous face in the grounds on a Saturday afternoon.

One of the biggest propaganda tools at this time was the poster campaign. Colourful, artistic, eye-catching and often humourous posters were plastered on every conceivable space. They covered every possible topic and appeared on hoardings, walls, shelters, railway stations, trains and buses. Their slogans became catch phrases such as 'Careless Talk Costs Lives', 'Be Like Dad – Keep Mum', 'Make

Above: The late Sir John Mills with his No. 1 fan, my friend Maureen Franklin, at his Denham home, 'Hill's House'. Sir John, who is holding the Academy Award he won for *Ryan's Daughter*, was kind enough to write the foreword to my book *Moviemania*.

Left: Mary Morris, co-star of *Pimpernel Smith* with Leslie Howard in 1941. Howard's plane was shot down in 1943 on a return flight from Lisbon, where he had been negotiating a deal to show British films. Afterwards, there was much speculation that the Germans had believed Churchill to be on board the plane. There were no survivors.

Yiewsley Town Hall during a salvage drive, displaying posters urging us to save paper, metal and rags. The young lad with his barrow appears to be setting a good example.

Yiewsley housewives in Castle Avenue responding to the call to save food scraps for pigs and poultry. The council's collector (left) is Benny Jones.

'Do and Mend', 'Dig For Victory' and 'Is Your Journey Really Necessary?' Recruitment posters for the armed forces, Civil Defence and Women's Land Army proved highly successful – the latter attracting 80,000 applicants. Comic cartoon-like characters 'Doctor Carrot' and 'Potato Pete' urged children to eat more vegetables, while the monster-like 'Squander Bug' warned us against waste of any kind. Even 'Desperate Dan' from the *Dandy* comic appealed to his readers to salvage waste paper, and my younger brother Michael heeded the advice as he collected old newspapers with a school friend. Most people tried to make some contribution to the war effort ranging from waste food (collected by pig farmers) to old clothing, frying pans, saucepans, scrap metal and even rags and bones.

The government constantly urged us to invest in National Savings, while the Local Authority asked us to contribute to various funds such as the Uxbridge District Comforts Fund, for which a street collection was made on 5 July 1941. Other regular fund raising schemes included an Uxbridge 'Spitfire Fund', 'War Weapons Week', 'Warship Week', 'Salute The Soldier Week' and the 'Wings For Victory' campaign.

The town was now full of uniformed men and women as more and more people were called to the colours. Some were stationed nearby; many were on embarkation leave; most would not be around for a very long time to come. Sadly, others would never return. Aside from the 'boys in blue' from the RAF camp who had been a familiar sight in Uxbridge since the First World War, we now saw a different blue uniform – that of wounded men from the RAF Hospital, who wore light-blue flannel suits, white shirts and bright red ties. There were also pilots with horrifically scarred faces, convalescing after undergoing plastic surgery at burns units.

In the absence of so many men at war, the role of women was of paramount importance, and all over the country thousands became engaged in what was commonly called 'war work'.

A Messerschmidt ME 109 displayed on waste ground in Bakers Road to boost the 'Spitfire Fund' launched in September 1940. The appeal realised over £3,250.

A most colourful display, including Allied flags, adorns the Yiewsley Town Hall to promote 'Salute the Soldier' week in April 1944.

The Duke of Norfolk, presenting the 'Bledisloe Cup' to Cllr Wilfred Roberts at the Central Hall, Yiewsley. The trophy was won by Yiewsley and West Drayton for their output in the national 'Dig For Victory' campaign of 1943.

Above: Medical Officers at the RAF Hospital, Uxbridge in 1941.

Left: An RAF Hospital staff nurse and sister outside the Sister's Mess in 1941.

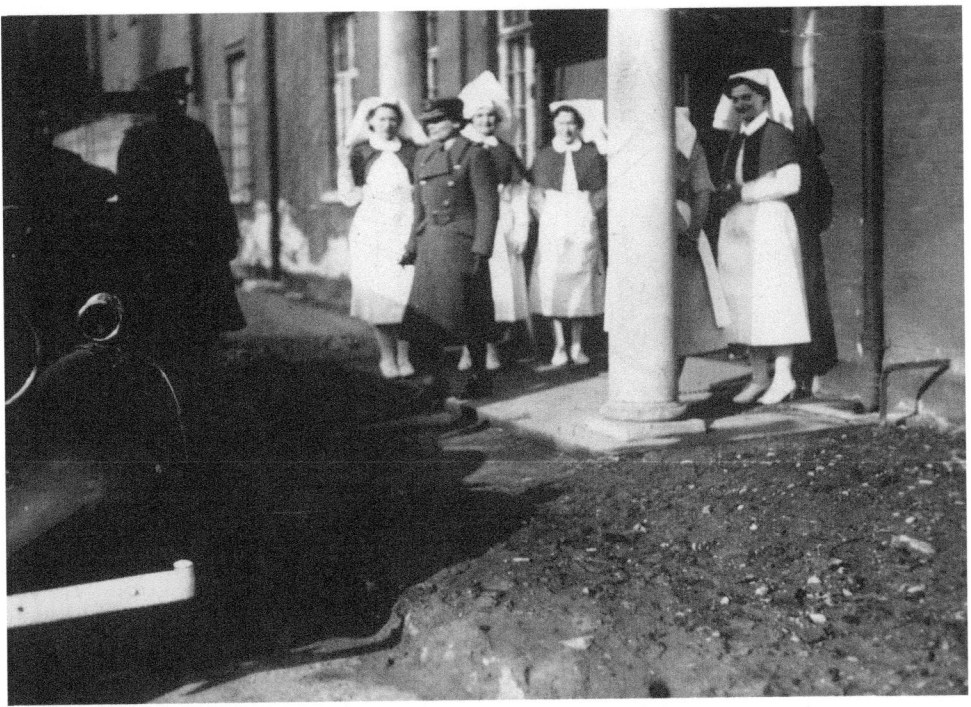

HRH the Duchess of Gloucester leaving the hospital following a visit in 1942.

Yiewsley and West Drayton ambulance crews. In front of the second ambulance on the right are Eva Buckingham (in white cap) and driver Val Lynch who, later, would lose her Army husband in tragic circumstances.

The drivers and nurses lined up in Whitethorn Avenue, Yiewsley. The team leader (centre) is Mr Griggs, almost completely outnumbered by the ladies on 'war work.'

Nurse Eva Buckingham (right) with her driver Ethel Squires. Later, Eva joined the ATS and served overseas.

Ambulance nurses, left to right: Violet Metcalfe, 'Tommy' Gardiner (whose brother was killed in France) and Eva Buckingham.

Those who were not serving in the women's branches of the three Armed Forces played a vital part by working in aircraft and munitions factories or on farms in the Women's Land Army (WLA). Others became ambulance drivers, air-raid wardens, railway porters, ticket collectors, bus conductresses (known as 'clippies') and postwomen, while some took over milk, bread and greengrocery rounds. In addition, the ladies of the Women's Voluntary Service (WVS) and Red Cross did sterling welfare work of all kinds.

The residents of How's Road and adjoining How's Close made a significant contribution to the war effort, and none more so than my lifelong friends the Burgoyne family, whose three sons and only daughter all enlisted in the services. The eldest, Brian, volunteered for the Army at the outbreak of war, and after two years in Iceland, joined the Special Operations Executive (SOE) in Algeria. Returning to their Baker Street London HQ, he became a Staff Sergeant engaged in administration work involving secret agents, the resistance movement in France and other Nazi occupied countries. His brother Denis, conscripted in September 1939, was posted to Greece in January 1941, then Crete and finally Egypt. He joined the 8th Army in the desert, taking part in the North Africa campaign, and did not return home from the Middle East war zone until July 1945. The youngest son, Patrick, enlisted in the Royal Artillery in December 1942, qualified as a signaller, and for the next four years served in Kenya, Ceylon (now Sri Lanka), Burma (with the 14th Army), India, Italy and Germany before being demobbed in May 1947. Not to be outdone by her brothers, the baby of the family, Sheila, joined the Women's Royal Naval Service (WRNS) as soon as she was old enough in May 1944, and worked on the Enigma decoding project, whose HQ was at Bletchley Park.

The first and, mercifully, only casualty from our road was Robert Heaney. Bob, one of my mother's schoolfellows, had joined the Royal Navy at the tender age of fifteen during the

Above: Hillingdon Village air-raid wardens, including five ladies, at their Cemetery Lodge HQ. Among the group are Patrol Leader Pat Read and Messrs Hawkins, Bignell, Sheepwash, Thompson, Osbourne, Underwood, Bridgeman, Clark, Bonney, Gauss and Reverend Bashford of St John's Church.

Left: The Burgoyne family in May 1940. Back row, left to right: Brian, Patrick and Denis. Front row: Gerald, Ethel and Sheila. Brian and Denis were on leave from the Army, prior to going overseas.

Right: Patrick Burgoyne in 1943, shortly before his posting to Kenya.

Below: Patrick and mutual friend Tony Gorman on embarkation leave. Previously with the 'Metesco' Home Guard, Tony served on the aircraft carrier HMS *Indomitable*, most aptly named as she was bombed and torpedoed several times, but survived until being 'scrapped' in 1955.

Left: Sheila Burgoyne (right) with Pat Holloway (left) and a WRNS colleague in March 1945.

Below: Petty Officer Robert Heaney (second from left in middle row), a family friend, killed by enemy action in December 1940.

This scroll commemorates

Mr. R. Heaney, Boatswain A/S
Royal Navy

held in honour as one who served King and Country in the world war of 1939-1945 and gave his life to save mankind from tyranny. May his sacrifice help to bring the peace and freedom for which he died.

Right: This Admiralty certificate sent to Bob's family says it all.

Below and overleaf: Bob's daughter Maureen's identity card. Everyone was bound by law to register and carry the card at all times.

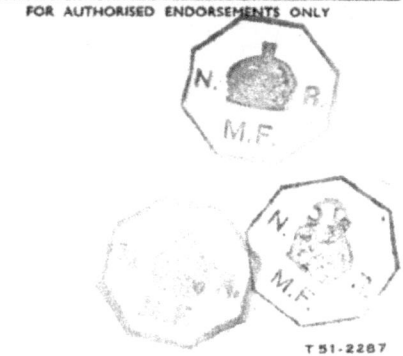

NUMBER		SURNAME	
BVAC	203 . 2	HEANEY	

CHRISTIAN NAMES (First only in full)

MAUREEN

CLASS CODE

13 312

FULL POSTAL ADDRESS

10 HOWS CLOSE

UXBRIDGE, MIDDX

BVA

HOLDER'S SIGNATURE

Maureen Heaney

CHANGES OF ADDRESS. No entry except by National Registration Officer, to whom removal must be notified.

REMOVED TO (Full Postal Address)

MARKING OR ERASURE, IS PUNISHABLE

First World War. During a distinguished career, he served on twenty-four different ships, received the Long Service and Good Conduct Medal, plus three Good Conduct Badges. He reached the rank of Petty Officer and on 9 September 1940 was promoted to Temporary Acting Boatswain on the destroyer HMS *Acheron*. Three months later, on 17 December 1940, Bob was killed in action when his ship sank after striking a mine off the Isle of Wight.

Living next door to the Burgoynes was the Alders family. Squadron Leader Alders was a peacetime RAF officer who, later in the war, became Officer Commanding troops on troopships in the Mediterranean. One of his sons, Leslie, became an Army Major, and the other, Wilfred, a Flight Sergeant in the RAF. My next door neighbour, Reg Bray, was a Major in the Royal Army Ordnance Corps and served in West Africa, while Don Hancox, who lived opposite, ended his army career as a Brigadier. His brother Reg, a well-known Uxbridge Cricket Club umpire, served with the RAF in India.

Other Army men from How's Close were Alf Sharp and Edward Moore, who was invalided out due to poor health and died later in Hillingdon Hospital. Ted Jones was in the Royal Marines and served on HMS *Warspite*, while another female member of the forces was Renee Castle in the Auxiliary Territorial Service (ATS). Others who were too old for military service, included Eddie Gifford (Home Guard), Ossie Palmer (AFS) and our landlord Mr Tomlins (ARP warden).

At the other end of the spectrum, there were four youths, including myself, who were too young. We were conscripted soon after the war ended.

Two years after the founding of the Air Training Corps (ATC) in February 1941, our school formed its own squadron, which we were encouraged to join at the age of fifteen. Training took place on two or three days a week, and after lessons ended at 4.00 p.m. the quadrangle became a parade ground where we practised squad drill (a polite name for square bashing). Then it was back to the classroom to learn aircraft recognition and how to send and receive messages in Morse Code. During the summer of 1943, 93,000 cadets nationwide spent a week at various

Right: My wife's cousin Able Seaman Joe Bateman of Yiewsley, joined the Royal Navy as a naval gunner in 1941, then volunteered for DEMS (Defensively Equipped Merchant Ships), seeing service in the Atlantic and Pacific. In 1942, his ship was torpedoed off the coast of north-west Africa, but miraculously, all the crew survived. After walking 10 miles through the jungle, he arrived at an American base where he was hospitalized before returning to England on sick leave.

Below: By a strange coincidence, Joe was then reunited with his great friend Reg Batchelor (on left) from Uxbridge, also on sick leave after being wounded during the Army's North Africa campaign. Later Joe was posted to the Far East, and eventually demobbed in Australia in 1946. He then married and made his home there.

Left: Another local family whose three sons all enlisted in the forces – The Egglestons of West Drayton. Left to right: Reg (RAF) Ted (REME) and Cyril (RAF Police) with their mother in 1943. Ted was a former member of West Drayton Home Guard.

Below: Wg Cdr T.L. Carthew, Regional Commandant of the ATC, inspected the Uxbridge 14F (founder) squadron at their Greenway School HQ on 16 November 1941. On the left he is seen presenting proficiency certificates to one of seventeen successful cadets. Mr H.A. Leno is in the background. On the right, Sir Gilfrid Craig JP, the squadron's president, looks on.

RAF stations, and our squadron was detailed to an Elementary Flying Training School (EFTS) at Shellingford in Berkshire. Here we practised parachute jumping from a high tower inside a giant hangar and had lessons in a simulated aircraft cabin called a 'Link Trainer', as well as physical training and aircraft-recognition classes. However, the highlight of the week was a thirty-minute flight in a Tiger Moth, the main basic training plane used during the war years. In the Nissen huts around the airfield's perimeter track, the RAF trainee pilots were waiting to go up, so, naturally, we had to wait our turn. We needed to borrow flying jackets, helmets and goggles from them, and also parachutes, which they were reluctant to part with, even for half an hour. Not having flown before, I found it exhilarating when the engine spluttered into life and a pungent reek of fuel filled the air. Then, with a deafening roar, the two-seater biplane took off. After a while the pilot (in the front cockpit) asked if I would like him to perform any aerobatics and suggested looping the loop. I agreed, and as we went into a steep climb, I found that, in an open cockpit, the air pressure was so intense that at the start of the loop I blacked out momentarily until the plane turned full circle and came right way up again. Later that summer we were airborne again – flying in an Avro Anson from RAF Halton, Bucks. Nothing so exciting this time however, as six of us sat on the floor of the fuselage, very cramped – and not one parachute between us! Needless to say there were no stunts, either.

During the school's summer break in August 1943, I took a holiday job at the Lowe & Shawyer Nurseries to earn some extra pocket money. Lowe & Shawyer, founded in 1852, had become the largest cut-flower nursery in the country by 1938, employing up to 1,400 workers in the summer months. Previously on 25 April 1934, it was honoured by a visit from HM Queen Mary accompanied by her granddaughter Princess Elizabeth, our present Queen.

With the outbreak of war in 1939, regulations compelled the nurseries to switch from flower to food production and by 1942, they had grown 1,326 tons of tomatoes plus 600 tons of other

Lowe & Shawyer's workmen during their lunch break at the nursery in 1947. Among them is Leonard Pitman, well-known local organ and piano teacher.

vegetables. Eighty employees had joined the Services, so I was put on tomato picking to try and maintain production! For three weeks, I did nothing but that from 7.30 a.m. to 5.30 p.m. until I felt that I never wanted to see another tomato. Nevertheless, I was still grateful to be given 'freebies' to take home at the end of each week.

Apart from providing the nation with a much-needed boost to food production, the nursery had inadvertently helped to save the 11 Group HQ at RAF Uxbridge from air attacks. It transpired later that the Luftwaffe aircrews had often been misled by the enormous areas of greenhouse glass which from the air appeared as large expanses of water – not shown on their maps! In fact, the only bomb to fall on the RAF station was a landmine that became entangled in a tree some 50 yards from the underground Operations Room on 27 September 1940. It was safely defused and detonated the next day at Harefield.

From 1941, local councils had organised programmes of events from July to September, under the title 'Summer Holidays at Home', to coincide with the government's advice to the public not to travel away from home for their holidays. The entertainment on offer included such a wide range of events that most people were quite happy to comply.

The council schemes gave me the idea to provide some home entertainment of my own, so I took over my father's garden shed as a convenient venue for my entry into show business. Helped by my friend and neighbour Alan Johnston, I set up a Saturday Matinee on 21 August 1943, and advance publicity was spread to neighbourhood children by word of mouth. And when, on the day, a queue formed in the alleyway to our back gate, I knew we were on a winner. The shed had been tidied up but was still fairly full of garden tools, bags of sand, cement and large pots of paint – which made

> URBAN DISTRICT OF U———E
>
> # PROGRAMME
> for
> ## SUMMER HOLIDAYS AT HOME
>
> As the Government do not wish persons to travel away from home for their holidays, the Council are arranging, in conjunction with local organisations, a series of holiday entertainments during the period commencing 13th July and ending 18th September
>
> *These Events will include:*
> THE R.A.F. MILITARY BAND, BICYCLE POLO MATCHES, BAND PERFORMANCES IN PUBLIC PARKS, OPEN-AIR CONCERTS, OPEN-AIR DANCING, PHYSICAL TRAINING AND GYM. DISPLAYS, DISPLAYS BY THE HOME GUARD, BOWLS DRIVES, SWIMMING GALAS, CONCERT AT THE CENTRAL HALL and a PERFORMANCE OF THE COMIC OPERA "MERRIE ENGLAND" AND OTHER ATTRACTIONS
>
> There will be some event every day of the week during the whole of the period and the detailed programme of events may be obtained, free of charge, on application to the Council Offices or to any of the A.R.P. Sub-offices throughout the district
>
> The Council earnestly hope that the public will avail themselves of the entertainment thus provided

Poster advertising the Uxbridge 'Holidays at Home' programme. Note that the town's name had to be abbreviated.

Above: One of the events included in the programme was this swimming gala at the Uxbridge Pool on 17 July 1943. The competitors were from youth and Scout groups.

Right: Original programme for my wartime concert in the garden shed on 21 August 1943.

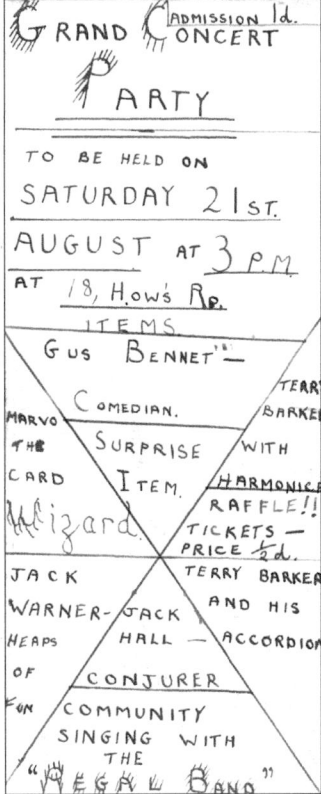

Cover of the song book published in conjunction with the Saturday-night radio programme that inspired some of the items in the show.

ideal seats. The floor at the back was a step higher than the front, so it became the stage, and a green curtain hung on a length of wire separated me from the audience. I had nailed a plank of wood above the door, and had painted, in bright red, 'Regal Shed' (named after the local cinema).

As I was to provide all the entertainment, Alan assumed the role of doorman, collecting the admission money of 1d each, and showing customers to their seats. As it was not very professional to come through the curtain (there was not room anyway) he shut the door and went round to a side window to tell me everyone was in. The programme, which I had handwritten on some fancy cards discovered in a local printer's bin, consisted of about six items, and naturally I used a different name for each act. During the interval we had a raffle (always popular, and a certain money-spinner) for the grand prize of a threepenny bit! Tickets were a mere ½d. My mother prepared a tray of glasses of lemonade made from a 1d packet of 'fizzy tablets', which my assistant handed out free to encourage ticket sales. The performance over, we eagerly counted the takings, then rushed to Woolworth's before closing time to buy some penny lead soldiers to add to our collections.

After a few performances, we began to get ideas above our station, so I extended the 'one man show,' roped in another three friends and went 'on the road' to Youth Clubs, garden fêtes and a Scout Gang show. Remember, we didn't have to compete with television in those days!

I left school at Easter, 1944, and joined Barclay's Bank as a junior clerk. The bank already employed three juniors, but within days one joined the Merchant Navy and another was conscripted to work in a coal mine. Because the mines had lost 36,000 workers to the forces by 1943, the Minister of Labour Ernest Bevin decreed that 10 per cent of all conscripts must be directed to the mines. As their fate was decided by ballot, they were known initially as 'ballottees', but soon became 'Bevin Boys' – for obvious reasons. In all, there were 48,000 of them including well-known personalities Eric Morecambe, Jimmy Savile and Brian Rix.

My first place of work, Barclay's Bank, undergoing an extensive modernisation programme many years after I left.

I soon discovered that working in a bank was not the cushy number that I'd been led to believe. My hours were from 8.30 a.m.-6.00 p.m, or later if the books hadn't balanced by then. My first duty was to load an ancient iron trolley with heavy, leather-bound ledgers in the basement and haul the load up to the ground floor in an old-fashioned manual lift. Then it was down to the vaults again to bring up an even heavier load of metal canisters full of cash. At the end of the day the procedure was repeated in reverse, and my lily-white hands soon became red raw!

There was a real Dickensian atmosphere about the place. The chief accountant sat on a tall, high-backed stool, writing at a high sloping desk, and wearing old white cuff protectors. He even used a black, solid wooden, cylindrical ruler for underlining. The bank dated from 1791, and I wondered if the old furnishings did too.

On Thursday mornings I accompanied the chief cashier to various branches on the outskirts of London, distributing bags of cash, and we were driven by the same chauffeur, Bert Burrows, who had taken our family to New Mill five years earlier. The weekly outing was a welcome break from tabulating cheques and postal orders on a hand cranked adding machine, but was less relaxing during the second half of 1944, when the Germans launched their flying bombs, especially around the London area.

I was paid the princely sum of £1 15s for my working week of 5½ days and, at the end of the year, was granted a rise of 4s.

Shortly after I had started my first job came one of the momentous days of the war – 6 June, 1944, or as it soon became known, D-Day. On that morning, an armada of over 5,000 vessels landed at five Normandy beachheads and at 6.20 a.m., Operation 'Overlord' (code name for the invasion) was under way. In the biggest combined military operation in history, some 200,000 Allied troops had landed by nightfall. Tragically up to 10,000 had perished in the process.

Amongst those who died that day was Capt. William Bowyer from West Drayton who had worked in the *Uxbridge Gazette*'s advertising department before the war. In January 1940, he enlisted in the Duke of Cornwall's Light Infantry, secured a commission, and volunteered for the Parachute Regiment, 6th Airborne Division, in 1943. Bill had married local girl and wartime ambulance driver Val Lynch in 1941. Later, long after the war was over, she discovered that her husband had been shot accidentally by his own batman. However, instead of harbouring any ill feelings, she told me that she 'had always felt so sorry for the poor man, having to live with that all his life.'

My cousin Ron Mellor was another of the many thousands who died in the Normandy campaign. His father had also fought in France during the First World War, and, after being severely wounded at Ypres, was sent to the RAF Hospital at Uxbridge to recuperate. It was here that he met and later married my father's sister. Their son Ron enlisted in the Royal Artillery in September 1939 at the age of seventeen and was killed on 30 June 1944. Apparently he had just taken cover in a dugout when it was hit by a shell. Nineteen-year-old Harold Ragsdale was with

Above left: Captain William Bowyer of West Drayton, who died on D-Day, 6 June 1944. A talented musician, he played the violin from the age of seven; was head soloist chorister at Eton, and played first cornet in the Yiewsley and West Drayton Silver Prize Band.

Above right: 'Bill' Bowyer and his wife Valentine Lynch after their wedding at St Catherine's, West Drayton on 21 June 1941.

Above left: My cousin Bombardier Ron Mellor, killed shortly after D-Day, two days after his twenty-second birthday.

Above right: Ron with his mother, my Aunt Jessie.

> 55, Greenland Cres.
> Southall,
> Middx
> June 28th 1944
>
> My own dearest Ron:
>
> Your birthday — & I can't give my sonny a nice big hug & be hugged in return. I am praying that this will be the last you will have away from us all.
>
> We sent you a few cigars & cards, I hope they arrived OK. Should have liked to have sent you a cake, but mustn't send anything eatable, so will make you an extra special one for when you come home dear & ice it too perhaps.
>
> Haven't heard from you since I received the letter-card on the 16th. am so looking forward to hearing from you. Are my letters coming through now.
>
> Mrs D. has had a letter from Doug — he is in action now.
>
> I earnestly hope all our dear friends will keep safe. It is a grand thing we have Cherbourg but it has been a hard fight — hasn't it.
>
> Many happy returns pet & a safe return soon.
> All our devoted love,
> Mum & Dad
> xxxx

Above left and right: Ron's last letter from his mother, which, sadly, arrived in France too late.

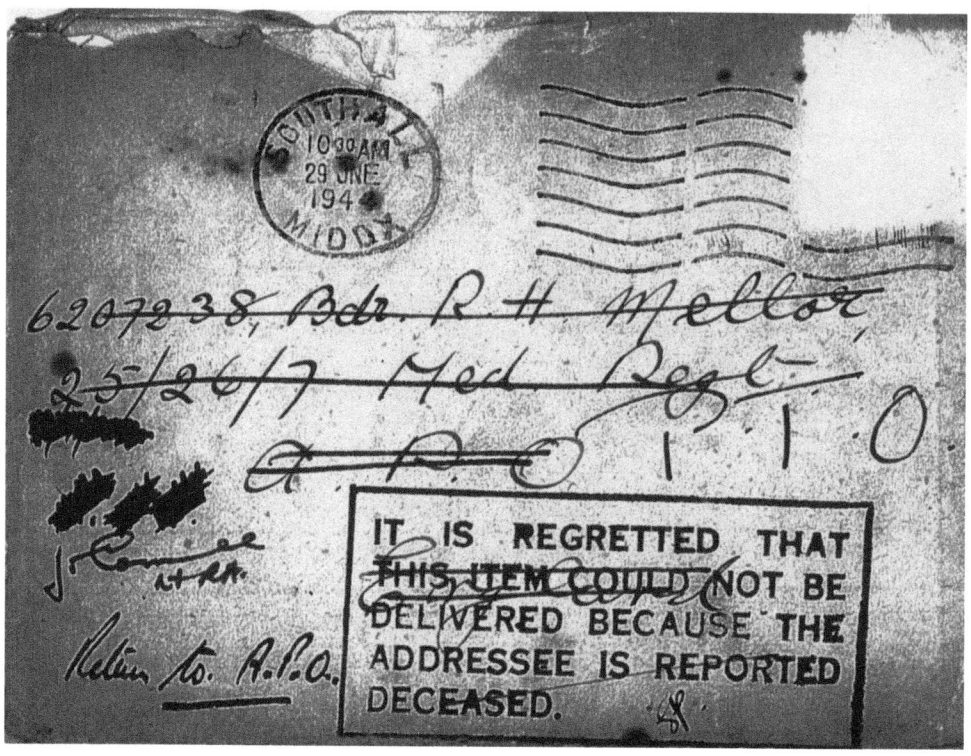

Above: The letter was returned with a stark message on the envelope.

Left: Ron's grave in the cemetery at Tilly-sur-Seulles, Northern France.

him and lost part of his leg and an arm. After being invalided out of the army, Harold visited Ron's family to give them the details of his death. He was buried at Tilly-sur-Seulles, south of Bayeux, home to another 4,000 British graves.

Some of the D-Day briefings of RAF aircrews had taken place at Uxbridge in the old camp cinema, the same building where T. E. Lawrence had once attended lectures, and where I enjoyed Saturday matinee pictures. Of course we had no idea of what was happening at the upper end of the High Street, just as, in the autumn of 1940, no one could have imagined how the course of history was being changed in the underground control centre on the other side of the camp.

Just after 7.00 a.m. on 22 June 1944, my father was on his way to work, sitting as usual on the upper deck of a 607 trolleybus from Uxbridge. It had just reached the top end of The Greenway when an unfamiliar object flew directly over the roof, causing the passengers to stand up and get a better view of what was one of Hitler's 'revenge weapons' – the V1 rocket, dubbed later as 'doodlebugs' or 'buzz bombs.'

At 7.10 a.m., district nurse Alice Dowden, a well-known local midwife, had returned home after a house call and was turning the key in the lock of her front door at the lower (western) end of The Greenway. Suddenly there was a mighty explosion as the flying bomb seen from the trolleybus landed on the four adjacent houses, killing seven people and injuring twenty-five. The blast had affected houses in surrounding streets, rendering forty-six uninhabitable, while another seventy-five needed major repairs. As for nurse Dowden, she suffered shock but was otherwise uninjured.

That evening, a telegram was delivered to Pamela Foster, who had been posted from 11 Group HQ at RAF Uxbridge to No.7 Maintenance Unit, RAF Quedgeley, Gloucester, in April 1944. The message told her that her parents Henry and Maud Foster had been in a serious accident, but after arriving back in Uxbridge, having caught a midnight train from Gloucester, she was told that, in fact, they had both died at No. 9 The Greenway. A wooden suitcase containing her mother's jewellery had been salvaged, and she retrieved it from a collection point in Whitehall Road. Pamela then visited the bomb site and, turning over some of the rubble, rescued one of her twenty-first birthday presents – a *Concise Oxford Dictionary*. Apart from the suitcase, it was the sole survivor from her former home, and sixty-four years on, it remains one of her treasured posessions.

The menace of the deadly German missiles continued until March 1945, by which time the V1 had been superseded by the more sophisticated V2. As with the Blitz, London was still on the receiving end, although a few fell in the local area, the worst incident occurring on 7 July 1944 when a V1 fell on a surface shelter at the Gramophone Co. in Hayes, killing thirty-seven workers and injuring eighty others.

In total, the rockets had accounted for over 6,000 lives and 18,000 serious injuries. They were also responsible for another evacuation of children from the London area.

It took the Allies almost a year to reach Berlin, for although the Germans were in retreat they offered stubborn resistance until the bitter end. Thus, there was a heavy price to pay for the Normandy campaign, and over 38,000 Allied war graves bear witness to the fact.

Finally, on Monday 7 May 1945 came the German surrender and it was time to put the flags out. The next day was designated VE (Victory in Europe) Day and a two-day holiday was announced. There was singing in the streets and many people really did dance all night. St Margaret's Church arranged a thanksgiving service, which was relayed to crowds outside, and on Sunday 13 May another service was held at Fassnidge Recreation Ground. Children's tea parties were hurriedly organised and on Saturday 12 May, trestle tables and benches were set up in the middle of streets throughout the area. Neighbours clubbed together to try and muster whatever goodies could be acquired 'off-ration', and some provided home-made cakes and jellies to give the kids a treat. Our street party took place in How's Close, with bunting strung

Bomb site in The Greenway after a V1 rocket demolished four houses on 22 June 1944. The seven residents killed were Henry and Maud Foster, Arthur and Frederick Borton, Peggy Dodd, Ethel Ware and her daughter Zena. The Anderson shelter seems to have survived.

Happy faces at the VE party held at the Co-op Hall in Windsor Street.

Another VE Day party at St John's Hall, St John's Road, for families living in the Uxbridge Moor area. This was the hall where we celebrated the 1935 Silver Jubilee and 1937 Coronation.

More VE Day celebrations, this one taking place in the playground of St Catherine's School, West Drayton.

Above: Having just enjoyed a tea party on trestle tables set up in Ferrers Avenue, West Drayton, the children and their parents were treated to a professional conjuring show as part of the VE Day festivities. The boy sitting next to the magician is ten-year-old Michael Briggs. Other spectators were Ruth Ingram, Robert Caughey, Philip Williams, Ken Briggs and four members of the Wisely family.

Left: This was the scene in Crosier Way, Ruislip, of even more VE celebrations on 12 May 1945. As well as their tea party, the youngsters all received a 'threepenny bit', a bag of sweets, and took part in a talent competition and fancy-dress parade.

The 'Welcome Home' sign displayed over the door of the Burgoyne family's house in How's Close in July 1945. Denis and Brian had just returned from overseas, although their brother Patrick was not demobbed until 1947. Sheila was on leave from the WRNS and standing next to her is family friend Leonard Kirby, who served in the Royal Navy and Merchant Navy from 1903-1924. During the Second World War he was a member of the Uxbridge Post Office Platoon of the Home Guard.

across the road from upstairs windows. In Wilmar Close, the revelry continued until the early hours. The residents had arranged a film show, games and races for the youngsters, followed by dancing up to midnight for the adults. One lad, aided by a few friends, dressed in drag and sang 'My Dreams are Getting Better all the Time' on a makeshift stage in the road. He was Ken Pearce – now a well-known Uxbridge historian.

On VE Day afternoon, Tuesday 8 May, I went to London with members of my Hillingdon Youth Club. After making our way down the Mall, we joined the milling 10,000 crowd outside Buckingham Palace, waiting for the King and Queen to appear on the balcony. Eventually, after the prolonged chanting of 'We want the King', the crowd's patience was rewarded when their Majesties stepped into view, accompanied by Princess Elizabeth in her ATS officers uniform, and Princess Margaret. Soon the chants began again and this time it was 'We want Winnie' until the hero of the hour duly appeared holding his trademark cigar and giving his now famous 'V' sign. The balcony party gave several encores, and the crowd began to disperse. This became quite a frightening experience, as we were carried and swept along for several minutes by the vast multitude of people.

The would-be peacemaker Neville Chamberlain did not live to see peace in his time, as sadly he had died from cancer on 9 November 1940. However his successor, Winston Churchill, acclaimed by many as the country's saviour, despite being labelled a warmonger by some of his opponents, was able to bask in the glory of victory. This, however, did not last for long. Even before the war ended in the Far East, a snap general election was called for 5 July 1945, and when the result was declared on 26 July, the Labour Party, led by Clement Atlee, swept to power with a landslide victory.

So, Churchill was out, rejected by a surprisingly fickle public who had idolised him during the war years, but now had visions of a brave new world – the new Jerusalem, a land flowing with milk and honey, which they thought might evolve with a socialist government. 'Winnie', as he had been affectionately known for six years, had made a return visit to Uxbridge while on the campaign trail. A tremendous crowd greeted his arrival as he was driven in an open car to the front of the Underground station. Dressed in a grey, pin-stripe suit, he made a short speech and gave his usual 'V' (for victory) sign. However, some onlookers, obviously not Churchill supporters, returned the sign the other way round. And in the subsequent election, the Labour candidate, Flt Lt Frank Beswick, easily defeated his Conservative rival, the Rt. Hon. J.J. Llewellyn, who had held the Uxbridge seat since 1929.

Meanwhile, the war in the Far East dragged on. There were more battles to be fought, more lives to be lost, more blood, sweat and tears. When the end finally came it was swift and sudden. The devastation caused by the dropping of two atomic bombs on the islands of Hiroshima and Nagasaki on 9 and 12 August 1945 brought about an immediate unconditional surrender by the Japanese. The 15 August consequently became Victory in Japan (VJ) Day, marking the cessation of all hostilities which had endured for six years less a few days.

The government declared another two-day holiday and the celebrations began all over again. Strangely enough, this time they were somewhat subdued and on a smaller scale, perhaps because of coming so soon after VE Day. Crowds still flocked to Buckingham Palace to cheer their Majesties, but, as autumn and the end of the year were approaching, the official Uxbridge celebrations were postponed until the following summer.

No matter – the war was finally over. We had peace at last, things would soon return to normal, and we could get on with our everyday lives again – or could we?

three

The Post-War Years

After the initial euphoria that followed VE and VJ day had died down, it was not long before we realised that nothing was going to change overnight, and that normality would not return for some time to come. In fact, many things got worse. There were shortages of food, fuel, coal – almost everything. Rationing and all the other restrictions continued; cuts were made in the meat, butter and margarine ration, and bread was rationed for the first time. The black market and the street corner 'spivs' were flourishing.

A general air of disillusionment prevailed, the wartime camaraderie was waning, and in their frustration people were complaining that 'It wasn't as bad as this when the war was on'. In many ways, they were right.

A series of unofficial strikes began one after the other. The dockers (43,000 of them) started the ball rolling, followed by road hauliers and milkmen. Even 2,000 RAF men serving abroad threatened to strike because of delays in demobilization, and then, to cap it all, footballers joined in while trying to secure a minimum wage of £7 per week.

Poster for the VJ Day celebrations, postponed from 1945.

To add to the mayhem, the country was in a dire financial crisis – practically bankrupt. And if all this didn't put a damper on the victory celebrations postponed by Uxbridge District Council until 8 June 1946, the weather certainly did. Continuous rain fell throughout the dismal Whit Saturday afternoon, as the procession moved along the High Street and Park Road to the swimming pool car park, where local clergy held a service of dedication and remembrance.

Most of the crowd who had turned out to witness the parade were sheltering under a sea of umbrellas or standing in shop doorways, but the unfortunate marchers, including Scouts, Guides, Cubs, Brownies and other organisations, must have been saturated by the time they reached their destination.

By evening the rain had subsided, enabling a torchlight procession, bonfire and firework display to go ahead on Uxbridge Common. The Victory Queen, elected for the occasion, was Olive Walling, who as Olive Maunder had been the town's beauty queen of 1944.

A few months earlier, on my eighteenth birthday in February, a brown envelope marked 'OHMS' had dropped on our doormat along with the birthday cards – His Majesty had not forgotten my birthday! These were my call-up papers for the RAF, the terms of engagement being designated D of PE (Duration of Present Emergency). Of course, no one knew how long that might be.

At the time I was about to take part in an amateur play, so our producer telephoned the Air Ministry to ask if I could be excused until the show was over. In the kindness of their heart the Ministry deferred my call-up for ten days, and as the Easter holiday was approaching, they tacked that on as well!

Finally, I was on a train from Euston to Lancashire, where I enlisted at Padgate. I was assigned to No 6 Flight B Squadron of the Recruitment Training Wing for eight weeks of square-bashing, rifle shooting and route marching. At Whitsun, we were given five days' leave – the first time we'd been allowed out of camp. Arriving at Euston by midnight, I caught an all night bus which terminated at Southall, then set off to walk the remaining six miles to Uxbridge. I had reached Hillingdon Hill when a kindly motorist offered me a lift into the town, and I arrived home at 3 a.m., where my mother was waiting up for me. In those days we did not get the 'key of the door' until the age of twenty-one.

After our passing out parade in July, I was posted to Kirkham, near Blackpool, to begin a pay-accounting course. We enjoyed every weekend off, invariably spent in Blackpool where we danced at the Winter Gardens to the music of Ted Heath, the biggest swing band of the day, or at the Tower Ballroom, where Reginald Dixon and other top organists were in residence.

One of the WAAFs on the course, Jasmine Maskelyne, who preferred to be called Bobbie, was the daughter of well-known magician Jasper Maskelyne, who in pre-war days had been a top-of-the-bill performer. In 1942, as an officer in the Royal Engineers, he was used as a camouflage expert during the Africa campaign in the Western Desert. With a selected team of craftsmen, he masterminded the construction of hundreds of 'dummy tanks' (outer shells made of light wood and cardboard) which, from the air, resembled the real thing. He even made them fire flashes and puffs of smoke to simulate shell fire. These decoys, along with other illusions created by Maskelyne, contributed in no small measure to the great British victory at El Alamein in early November 1942. General Montgomery's offensive began on 30 October and resulted in the German General Rommel's full retreat by 4 November. On Sunday, 15 November, church bells rang out throughout Britain for the first time since early 1940, to mark victory in the greatest battle of the war.

After completing the accounting course, I was granted ten-days leave before reporting to 29 Squadron, based at West Malling in Kent – a beautiful setting in the 'Garden of England'.

Part of the victory parade at the eastern end of the High Street.

With my pay-accounting course colleagues at Kirkham, Lancs. Bobbie Maskelyne (Jasper's daughter) is fourth from the right in the back row, next to me.

Unfortunately, my first introduction to this demi-paradise was not exactly pleasant. Travelling on the last train from Victoria late on a hot Saturday in August, I alighted at the wrong station (on the advice of a local man sitting in my compartment). As I crossed the bridge over the railway line, the station was suddenly plunged into darkness along with all the street lighting outside. It was 11.15 p.m.

The next five hours were spent trudging through the Kent countryside – apple orchards, hop fields and narrow lanes. There were no signposts and no one to ask for directions. Finally the weight of a full kit-bag on my shoulder plus a back and side pack forced me to call a halt on the edge of a wood, where I slept until dawn. I eventually found the airfield at 7.00 a.m. on Sunday morning.

West Malling airfield had opened as a private landing ground in 1930, and was taken over by the RAF in early 1940. It soon became a target for the German Luftwaffe, along with other areodromes in south-east England, and, from 10 August to the end of September 1940, was the victim of fourteen intense bombing attacks in which planes were destroyed and RAF and Army personnel killed. The station was out of action for several weeks, and not fully operational until the spring of 1941. Then, on 27 April, 29 Squadron (which I joined five years later) arrived at West Malling with new Beaufighters (night interceptor planes). One of their pilots was the legendary Guy Gibson, who was awarded the VC after leading the daring 'Dambuster' raid in May 1943. Prior to that, during his time at West Malling, 29 Squadron had shot down forty-nine enemy aircraft. In recent years, the airfield site has been developed by the local council, and the main road running through it has been named Gibson Drive, at the end of which stands a memorial and a statue of an unnamed airman.

During Gibson's time at the station, the landing area was still grass surfaced, and Sommerfield tracking had to be laid to provide all-weather serviceability. This was a portable metal track, named after its inventor John Sommerfield who lived in Cowley High Street. The first length was built in the back garden of his home 'The Cedars', with help from two neighbours, builder W.S. Try and general shopkeeper Mr Moth. By 1942 Mr Sommerfield was employing 600 people at his factory in Iver Lane. Among them was Alan Johnston, who had just left school and worked a forty-eight-hour week for which he was paid £1 8s. Eventually, more factories were set up on the continent and, after D-Day, the tracking was used extensively for roads and landing strips.

I had not been at West Malling very long before two new squadrons arrived. The first was 25 Squadron followed by 85 Squadron a few months later. Both were equipped with de Havilland night fighter Mosquitoes, which meant that all three squadrons were flying the same aircraft. This was 85 Squadron's third stay at West Malling, their first being in 1943 under the leadership of the famous Wing Commander John 'Cat's Eyes' Cunningham. 25 Squadron had arrived without a pay clerk, and I was transferred to fill the vacancy. I moved into their barrack block on the other side of the square, but still sat at the same desk in the Station Headquarters office.

I was able to get home to Uxbridge at weekends, except on the odd occasion when duty called. Guard duties sometimes occurred over a weekend, and each September, all the squadrons took part in a Battle of Britain parade at Hastings, Sussex, on the Sunday nearest to the 15th. In addition, one unexpected duty arose when the country was hit by one of the worst winters ever recorded. Starting in January 1947 and continuing through February and March, heavy snowstorms, non-stop blizzards and sub-zero temperatures brought Britain to a standstill. More strikes, countless power cuts, and food and fuel shortages added to the misery. A mile and a half from the camp at West Malling railway station, there were a few wagons full of coal – a vital commodity in the circumstances. It appeared, however, that the coal-lorry drivers were reluctant to negotiate the uphill journey to the airfield due to the treacherous road conditions. That left only one option – we would have to collect it ourselves, as supplies were fast running out. So several details armed with large shovels were driven to the station sidings, where the weekend was spent loading the lorries with the contents of the coal trucks in bitterly cold conditions. Thankfully, we were fortified with mugs of hot soup and tea from the urns we had brought with us.

Our reward for the extra duty was a forty-eight hour pass, and I managed to get to Uxbridge, although 300 roads were blocked and fifteen towns were still cut off throughout the country. My father met me at the Underground station with the sad news that my grandmother had just died. Being away, I had not realised she was ill, although she had suffered from chronic bronchitis for many years. When we reached home, I went into her bedroom where my mother lifted the sheet covering her body. She had always been short in stature, but I was surprised how small and shrivelled she looked in her big double bed. As I was due back at camp on Sunday night, I was unable to attend her funeral on the following Friday, 14 March, at Kensal Green cemetery, north-west London, where she was laid to rest in the same grave as her beloved husband, taken from her so tragically sixteen years earlier.

At last the horrendous winter gave way to spring, but not before the thaw caused severe flooding in many parts of the country. Soon followed one of the most glorious summers on record – a just reward for what we had endured earlier. My long-time friend Patrick Burgoyne had returned from Army service overseas, and was demobbed in May 1947. He spent much of his demob leave at Lord's cricket ground, and I was able to join him on occasional leaves. This was to be a golden summer for Middlesex C.C., who won the County Championship, and in particular for their great batsman Denis Compton, who we felt privileged to watch on his way to breaking two all-time records. By the end of the season, he had notched up eighteen centuries and a total of 3,816 runs.

The long, hot summer went on and on. So did the economic crisis and austerity cuts. The meat ration was reduced to one shilling's worth a week, and potatoes were rationed to 3lbs per person per week. Pleasure motoring and foreign holidays were banned completely.

One bright event brought some cheer to the nation, however. The Royal Wedding of Princess Elizabeth and Prince Philip, Duke of Edinburgh took place on 20 November 1947. It was the most glittering occasion since the 1937 Coronation. The government had awarded the Princess extra clothing coupons for her wedding dress, designed by Norman Hartnell, but clothes rationing continued until 1949. It had lasted for eight years.

Meanwhile, changes had taken place at West Malling. A number of German prisoners of war had been working on the camp for some time, and were now repatriated. Not, however, before they had beaten our station football team in a challenge match on Town Malling's ground. The game was played on a bone-hard snow-packed pitch during the freeze, and their superior fitness took us by surprise. The station was then 'de-WAAFed' – an RAF expression for posting all WAAF personnel to other locations, leaving a 'men only' zone.

I had not been inside the Uxbridge RAF camp since before the war, as it had been closed to the general public for the duration. However, in 1948, I had two opportunities to visit – firstly accompanying the West Malling football team to compete in an inter-group cup tie on the depot ground, where once we watched Uxbridge FC play. The second occasion was to attend a boxing tournament staged in the gymnasium (formerly the camp cinema). In fact, with our Flight Sergeant's permission, I skipped the fights and spent a night at home before returning to Kent by an early morning train.

With fellow members of 25 Squadron at West Malling. In the centre of the back row is Peter Dilorenzo, who became a football commentator with ITV under his new name of Lorenzo.

Council chairman W.E. Black receiving the Olympic Torch from RAF Corporal Dafter, before it was carried on to Wembley, prior to the 1948 Olympics.

August 1948 saw the first renewal of the Olympic Games since the 1936 event in Berlin. Billed as the London Olympics, the main venue was at Wembley, with Henley, Cowes and Bisley in supporting roles. Uxbridge played its part in the lead up to the opening ceremony when the Olympic flame was carried through the town on 29 July. Starting from Dover, it reached the Bucks-Middlesex border at Long Bridge around 2.00 p.m., where the chairman of the council, W.E. Black JP, accepted the torch from Cpl E. Dafter of RAF Halton. It was then taken over by A.L.M. Phipps of Thames Valley Harriers who carried it via Windsor Street and Park Road to the next changeover on the Western Avenue.

I, of course, missed the event – and the sequel, an unscheduled performance by my eight-year-old brother Kevin who, according to reliable witnesses, entertained the residents of How's Road and How's Close with his own re-enactment of the ceremony. Correctly attired in singlet, running shorts and plimsolls, while carrying aloft a home-made torch, he ran around the block several times until completely exhausted. His 'Olympic' torch was a stick atached to a Nescafé tin stuffed with a paraffin-soaked rag, and then set alight.

Back in the real world, Uxbridge had another part to play in the games. The swimming pool was used by the Olympic teams for practice, and the RAF camp acted as an Olympic village for a time by housing many of the competitors. Another 700 athletes were based at RAF West Drayton. Most importantly, the town had its own representative at the games in the person of racing cyclist Lewis Pond, son of Windsor Street baker, James Pond. Lew, who had finished second in the Grand Prix d'Europe in 1945 and captained English teams on many foreign tours, was a member of the British Olympic team.

A fortnight after the games, my number came up. Not in the tragic sense, of course – merely my service group, No. 74, otherwise known as my 'demob number'. On 1 September 1948, I travelled from Kent to No. 101 PDC (Personnel Dispersal Centre), based at my old haunt of Kirkham. After

dinner, it was on the bus to Blackpool for one last look round – then an early night in readiness for the big day. Quite a busy day too, trailing around various sections, collecting signatures on different documents – then finally, the moment everyone looked forward to – being kitted out with 'civvies'. The stores staff were ready with all the usual wisecracks. If anyone was a bit fussy, it would be 'What do you think this is – Savile Row?!'

I selected a plain suit, grey striped shirt with two detachable collars, Paisley-patterned tie that clashed violently with the shirt, a green trilby hat that I never wore, a pair of brown shoes and a light raincoat. We were also allowed to keep our battledress blouse, trousers and greatcoat. Most ex-servicemen had their coats dyed a dark colour, after removing the flashes and buttons, so they could be worn in 'civvy street'. I used mine as an extra covering on my bed. Very cosy!

By early afternoon I was on the train to London and then home, wearing the King's uniform for the last time and clutching my new wardrobe, which was wrapped in a brown-paper parcel tied up with string – the tell-tale sign of someone just demobbed. Once back in 'civvy street', I decided to enjoy the whole of my eight weeks demob. leave before looking for a job. That proved to be a big mistake as jobs were few and far between. My first interview was at a well- known local estate agents, where I was seen by the boss. When I told him that I had just been demobbed after two and a half years in the RAF, he asked what rank I was. I said 'Corporal', to which he replied rather smugly 'Oh, really – I was a Major myself'. At that point I sensed that the interview was going nowhere, and I was right. At the end, he criticised my clothing (brown overcoat and shoes, yellow scarf) which to me seemed quite normal – after all, it was November. He then advised me that the correct way to dress for an interview was in a dark suit, well-polished black shoes and a white collar and tie. Perhaps he had not heard of clothes rationing, and, in any event,

Opposite above: As I was in uniform, future wife Joy (on extreme right) decided to 'do her bit' and worked as a ward orderly at Hillingdon Hospital.

Opposite below: A change of costume for both of us when attending the premiere of *Rope* at the Carlton, Haymarket. Also pictured left to right: D.A. Denyer, assistant manager of our Regal cinema, an official from Transatlantic Pictures and Vic Swain, journalist on the *Uxbridge Gazette*.

Right: My Gunnersbury classmate Kenneth Haigh at the start of his acting career.

I possessed only one suit – the light grey, rather ill-fitting demob issue supplied courtesy of the RAF two months previously. I left the office contemplating that the eventual outcome would be a blessing in disguise.

Staying with estate agents, my next port of call was at Harold Leno's High Street office. A former chairman of Uxbridge Council, Harold was an old school friend of my fathers. Unfortunately he had no vacancies at the time. After that, I answered a local newspaper advertisement for a wages clerk in a coal company's office attached to Vine Street railway station. This time the interview went reasonably well. However, the manager had one reservation – that in view of my youth (approaching twenty-one) I might not be able to cope with any 'trouble from the men'. I presumed he meant that if their wages were incorrect, they might turn nasty! However, when I told him that in the RAF, I had handled the pay for a whole squadron up to and including the rank of Warrant Officer, he sent me for a second interview at the company's Head Office in London. Unfortunately, once again it was a 'No.'

By now feeling a trifle despondent, I was cheered up considerably when attending a former classmate's twenty-first birthday party at The Angel in Hayes. His father had hired a couple of cabaret acts and the star performer, who kept us in fits of laughter, was an unknown young comedian. His name was Benny Hill. I then had a lucky break – well two lucky breaks really. Firstly, I was fortunate enough to win a competition organised by the Regal Cinema for writing notes on a new film – Alfred Hitchcock's 'Rope'. The prize was dinner for two at London's Café Royal and complimentary tickets for the film's premiere at the Carlton, Haymarket afterwards. Then, a few days later, I was offered a position of costing clerk with a Harefield company. My starting wage was £4 10s, rising to £5 after a three-month trial period. Things were looking up!

One Saturday morning in early February 1949, I was due to meet my fiancée, Joy, and help choose her engagement ring, when a surprise visitor arrived on the doorstep. It was my former Gunnersbury schoolmate Kenneth Haigh, just demobbed from the Army. We hadn't seen each

The Old Dock at Fountain's Mill, a favourite fishing haunt of Mark's and countless others. Anglers are strangely absent from this picture of a sketch artist at work in between the canal dock on the left and the River Frays on the right as it flows under the High Street from the floodgates.

The war is over but times are far from normal. Cars on the roads are a rarity and cyclists in Windsor Street have it almost to themselves.

Rationing and shortages still abound and queues are ongoing. This one is for coke at the Uxbridge Gas Works off Cowley Mill Road.

other for three years. I introduced him to Joy, then the three of us adjourned to the Express Dairy cafeteria for morning coffee. We had a lot of catching up to do, and two hours and several coffees later, it was time to visit the jeweller. Ken told us that he was applying for a scholarship to the Central School of Speech and Drama, as he was determined to pursue an acting career. Before long, he secured the title role in a television production of *Golden Boy*, followed by film parts in *High Flight* with Ray Milland, *My Teenage Daughter* with Anna Neagle and Sylvia Syms

Left: Ex-St Mary's schoolbly Mark (Taggart) McMannus.

Below: Uxbridge Football Club, all smiles after settling in at their new ground, 'Honeycroft', in Cleveland Road. Left to right, back row: Owen, Morse, Andrews, Rees, Poole, Sutch. Front row: Morgan, Poxon, Needham, Parham, Sheppard.

and Otto Preminger's *Saint Joan*. His career really took off when he played the original 'angry young man' in John Osborne's *Look Back in Anger* at the Royal Court Theatre and then on Broadway.

At the same time, another budding young actor was attending my former junior school, St Mary's. A classmate of my brother Adrian, his name was Mark McManus. He eventually achieved worldwide fame in the television series *Taggart* over a period of eleven years. He told me later at a school reunion how much he had enjoyed his schooling at St Mary's, and paid tributes to his (and my) teachers Molly Duffy and Madge Daly. He also loved to go fishing in the Old Dock at Fountain's Mill after school hours. Sadly, he is no longer with us.

Now we were into the last year of the decade, a few rays of hope in the shape of home comforts appeared on the horizon. Clothes rationing was finally abolished on 15 March 1949, sweet rationing was granted a temporary reprieve – albeit for only four months, and the price of beer was reduced by 1d a pint.

Sadly, it wasn't all good news. The milk ration was reduced, the price of petrol was increased to 2s 3d per gallon, and the pound was devalued drastically by over 30 per cent. The dockers were also on strike again.

Since my demob. I had been able to resume my role as a regular supporter of Uxbridge Football Club, which, in September 1948, had acquired a permanent ground of its own for the first time. This was located at Honeycroft in Cleveland Road, and had been secured through the good offices of businessman Jack Hutton and builder W.S. Try who purchased the adjoining house for £5,800 for use as a clubhouse and dressing rooms. A highlight of one of their opening games at the new ground was a victory over Wycombe Wanderers in the FA Cup before a 4,000 crowd. A boyhood friend of pre-war days, the late Roger Parham, was a regular in the side, playing at inside forward, and a year or so later I renewed my acquaintance with him when I joined Harefield Cricket Club, where he was an opening fast bowler.

In September 1949 it was FA Cup time again and Uxbridge had a home tie against Chesham on Saturday 17th, kick-off 3.15 p.m.. As it happened this was the same day, and exact time, of our wedding which, of course, had been planned months in advance. When I saw the fixture list in the *Uxbridge Gazette*, I jokingly suggested to the bride-to-be that perhaps I should get my priorities right and rearrange the wedding time in order to see the match, but she failed to appreciate my sense of humour. The 17 September was her 21st birthday – exactly nine years to the day from the ill-fated City of Benares sinking, an ordeal that she had avoided at the last minute.

As a wedding present, my new firm awarded me an extra increase of 25s per week, bringing my total wage to £6 5s. That is how I started married life. Rationing was still in force, but somehow we managed to hold a modest reception, the wedding breakfast being bolstered by several tins of fruit and Australian ham – a welcome change from wartime spam. They were a gift from my mother-in-law's sister, who had emigrated to Australia when the war ended.

And now it was time to move on. Time to spread my wings and fly the nest. Time, in fact, to move from Uxbridge – albeit only a few miles away.

A new phase of my life was beginning as the first half of the century drew to its close, leaving me with some bitter-sweet memories of the past decade. A decade which included six years of war – the worst war in our history. A war which had claimed the lives of over 55 million people worldwide.

For many, the lyrics of the favourite wartime song 'We'll Meet Again' would never be a reality. For those who had lost loved ones, life could never be the same again. However, those of us who were more fortunate could at least look forward to a brighter future and savour the hard-won peace, as a new wind of change blew throughout the land.

Other local titles published by Tempus

Ickenham
JAMES SKINNER

This fascinating collection of old photographs of Ickenham is full of information about the village from its earliest time right through to its development into the busy suburb it is today. From images of Ickenham's buildings, such as Swakeleys and the Fox and Geese public house, to the well-known pond at the centre of the village, the vibrant social life of the area is conveyed here.

978 07524 3411 7

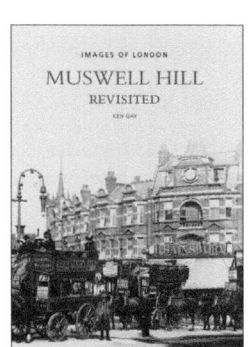

Around Uxbridge
JAMES SKINNER

This interesting volume provides a glimpse into the history of Uxbridge during the last century, capturing images of sport and recreation, education and religion, events and personalities as well as the local people who have lived and worked in and around Uxbridge. From early views of gas lamps and cobblestones to photographs of Uxbridge Football Club at the RAF stadium ground in the mid-1930s, and the growth of the manufacturing industry, this book will appeal to all those who are keen to discover what life was once like in this part of Middlesex.

978 07524 3205 2

Muswell Hill Revisited
KEN GAY

Muswell Hill was largely untouched by change until, in 1896, James Edmondson began to build the thirty acres of elegant shopping parades and tree-lined avenues transforming this sleepy Middlesex village into a prosperous Edwardian suburb. This collection conjures up a forgotten world of trams, horse-drawn buses and dances at the Grove. From the wedding of Maud Bailey in 1912 to Grand Avenue after an air raid, Alexandra Palace and the Muswell Hill Festival, all aspects of life in the area during the last century are recorded.

978 07524 3835 1

West Drayton and Yiewsley
JAMES SKINNER

This compilation of over 200 old photographs illustrates the history of these two Middlesex towns, charting their progress from agricultural communities of golden cornfields, to the coming of the railways and industry, including brickmaking, gravel and ballast production. West Drayton was also once a centre of culture, with many authors, actors and artists choosing to live there.

978 07524 2841 3

If you are interested in purchasing other books published by Tempus, or in case you have difficulty finding any History Press books in your local bookshop, you can also place orders directly through our website

www.thehistorypress.co.uk